OUR SPIRITS CARRY OUR VOICES

West Oakland to West Africa Poetry Exchange

Reviews

"Our Spirits Carry Our Voices is a literary journey to define our own sense of place and identity through a dialogic riff between West Africans and West Oakland poets. Karla Brundage and Sir Black creatively lead their poetic teams to transcend technological space to come face-to-face with ancestral memories and current trans-Atlantic realities to become, as one poet imagines, "one in thought, in trauma, in heritage, in Hope."

-**Halifu Osumare,** Author of The Hiplife in Ghana: West African Indigenization of Hip-Hop(2012) and Dancing in Blackness, a Memoir(2018)

"In 2017, a group of Oakland poets and a group of West African poets wrote poems together for a year. And at the end of that year, the Oakland poets travelled to Ghana to hold a slam. Our Spirits Carry Our Voices tells the story of this journey through prose and poetry. Part travelogue, part celebration this is a beautifully written collection, one optimistic about the ability of poetry to bring people together and share histories."

-**Juliana Spahr** is a professor of English at Mills College and the recipient of the 2009 Hardison Poetry Prize.

"Our Spirits Carry Our Voices is significant on many levels. It is a verification of the possibility of connections in a turbulent world. The presence of mostly African American and African voices reflecting on common themes such as the African Diaspora, identity, family, and the visible and invisible worlds, shows the power of partnering, interconnectedness, and enhanced understanding between cultures, histories and reflections. The responsible reader will recognize the rich resources of the huge and ancient continent of Africa, and how Africans were essential and indispensable to the building and prosperity of capitalism, the USA and Europe."

-**Kathryn Takra, Phd.** Winner of the American Book Award

WO2WA Poetry Partners

Editor's Note: The sequence of the collection reflects the exchange between partners and features the Renshi poetry style by bolding the last line of each poem which is subsequently the first line of their partner's response poem- creating a linked conversation. Each partner pair submitted one sequence of four poems that make up the chapters.

Z.Afua and Imani
Nathaniel and Radhiyah
Obi and Makeda
Nathaniel and Xiomara
Crystal and Wild-Flower
Joseph and Zakiyyah
Mariska and Wanda
Emmanuel and Adeshima
WhoIsDeydzi and Tamaris
Jewell and Tyrice
Xorlarli and Sara
Azi and Mimi
Sir Black and Karla

West Oakland to West Africa Poetry Exchange

Exchange partners meet at Agoo Hostel

Makola Market

OUR SPIRITS CARRY OUR VOICES

West Oakland to West Africa Poetry Exchange

Edited by Karla Brundage

© 2019

Pacific Raven Press, LLC

Ka`a`awa, Hawai`i 96730

ISBN 978-0-9993039-7-9

Cover art by Nana Boatang

Photography by Wanda Sabir and CriboutTV

Photo Editor Tyrice Deane Brown

Book Layout by Eien Design **www.eiendesignstudio.com**

Editor: Karla Brundage

Contributing editors: Mera Moore, Allison Francis

Advisory: Tyrice Deane Brown, Zakiyyah G. E. Capehart, Sandra Hooper Mayfield, Wanda Sabir, Crystal Tettey, Yibor Kojo Yibor

This work is licensed under Pacific Raven Press, LLC

Library of Congress Cataloging-in-Publication Data

Our Spirits Carry Our Voices by Karla Brundage

Catalogued as: Poetry, African, African American, History, Travel, Culture

Printed in the United States of America

Pacific Raven Press, LLC, is an independent publisher

PO Box 678 Ka`a`awa, HI 96730

pacificravenpress@yahoo.com

http://pacificravenpress.co/

Dedication

Sankofa-Let Us Return

This is book dedicated to our African ancestors who crossed the Atlantic in the great *maafa,* the calamity also known as the Middle Passage. To those who died, to those who are present and to those who will make the journey home, the *sankofa* journey, to the motherland. To those who became part of the Americas, and those whose seed created this grand diaspora. To those who are with us and those who hold their bitterness cursing from their graves. To the spirits still walking the earth with good will, hoping to redirect those of us who are lost and wounded.

This book is also dedicated to all the artist activists including W.E. B. Du Bois, Malcolm X, Maya Angelou, and Muhammad Ali who gathered and took a journey home to the great country of Ghana and were welcomed through a Door of Return.

Table of Contents

Acknowledgments

Thank you to all the people who both contributed to this book and are named in this book: members of Ehalakasa and participants in WO2WA, West Oakland to West Africa. A very special thanks to our publisher Pacific Raven Press and Sir Black without whom this project could not have been possible, and to Tyrice Deane Brown who stood by this project from the day we created the acronym WO2WA in her dorm room.

Thank you to those who believed this could actually happen, and those who believed it could not (and there were many). Thanks also to Mills College from whom I received a Community Engagement Fellowship that enabled me the time to do this project while completing my MFA. Thank you Juliana Spahr for believing in my vision. Thanks to the City of Oakland for the Oakland Cultural Fund grant which helped support the printing of our chapbook. Thank you to many venues in Oakland including Maliki West African Restaurant and the Back Room where we held readings, West Oakland Branch Library where we met weekly for our writing workshop, Wanda Sabir and Wanda's Picks, Zakiyyah G.E. Capehart, KPFA radio for our international interview. Adeshima and Self Care Reform for spiritual and yoga guidance, Mama Makeda and Sugar Water,

Mimi Gonzalez for always believing in the project and its spirit no matter the obstacle, Sara Biel and Jay Trollinger for teaching us how to bind books and make the covers, Donte Clark for donation his showing of *Romeo is Bleeding* for our biggest fundraiser. Thanks to Chase Spears aka madamcjda3rd, a former student who emerged after her trip to Ghana and produced a beautiful video of our trip.

Thank you Benita Lubic and Travelaire for booking our trip. Our gratitude goes to Agoo Hostel in Accra where we created a haven to rest during our stay and One Africa and Seestah Imakus in El Mina. Thank you to all the bus drivers and people who helped us go from place to place safely. Chris Kofi of Positive Art Shop who serve as our personal tour guide for the entire trip, navigating difficult moments, sharing culture and giving us insights which is the greatest gift.

Thank you also to those who believed in this book project and worked many hours editing and suggesting Allison Francis and Mera Moore. And finally, thanks to my family, Kathryn Takara, poet writer, activist whose life journey has served as an inspiration to me. She also facilitated a WO2WA workshop. Thank you my daughter Asha Brundage-Moore whose grace and independence allows her mother to travel. Finally, thank you to my father who has taught me the skill of stubborn resistance.

Foreword

By Sir Black, aka Yibor Kojo Yibor
Co-Founder of Ehalakasa

It was a great joy for my team and me from West Africa to experience this unforgettable exchange with West Oakland under the able leadership of Karla in what was WO2WA, like every organism was conceived and birthed out of hope with the conviction of becoming something beautiful, regardless of how it turned out.

Here we are after months of discussions and correspondence; we have now something more than just beauty, we have a family, with amazing memories and experiences worth celebrating.

On behalf the entire Ehalakasa family, I would like to express my sincere gratitude to Karla for deciding to lead the narrow way for this exchange that is now gone broad with unlimited possibilities of what WO2WA can become. I believe this project could be channeled to bring more young people from West Oakland to West Africa to connect and exchange creatively, culturally, and spiritually all in the spirit of poetry.

The partnership between Ehalakasa and Karla's West Oakland team has developed over the period into something special to cherish and uphold. Initiated through emails, letter writing and ideas, we shared how to find and identify poets/writers, part-ner-pairing, exchanging poetry and stories via Skype meetings, discussions and performances until the final moment of seeing everyone face to face in Nima, Accra, Ghana in May of 2018.

It was all fun at the hotel where the West Oakland team were lodging. I still have memories of how they walked down the stairs with hope in their eyes, and our long hugging and tight hand- shaking with smiles coupled with joy when our two groups exchanged pleasantries in real life. I recall it had rained that morning and still drizzling; however, the Ehalakasa team managed to come simply because they were all excited and had been looking forward to this day with hope.

I believe the coming of WO2WA initiated some kind of revival and bonding in Ehalakasa because we have become more grounded as family. We have since experienced different dimen-sions of exchange and collaborations with several other institu-tions as a family compared to the usual individual shows.

I am convinced that a part of our growth in numbers, orga-nization and projects can be linked to the success story of host-ing WO2WA in Ghana. The visibility of the exchange online, our joint school workshop program, the visit to the old Accra city and the WOWA slam that saw Ehalakasa winning over the West Oakland with just a point.

I am confident that the partnership between Ehalakasa and Karla's West Oakland team will grow in the coming years, and that we will ensure our mutual benefit and advancement as a community for fruitful, future projects.

Introduction

By Karla Brundage

"Sweet, crazy conversations full of half sentences, daydreams and misunderstandings more thrilling than understanding could ever be."
— **Toni Morrison, Beloved**

Creating a poetry exchange between West Oakland and West Africa has been many years in the making. I worked with the idea of how rap is connected to the griot tradition and how initially hip-hop was a phoenix for the Black community to rise from the ashes, fists first. Long before Wakanda, and many years after the Ten-Point Program of the revolutionary Black Panther Party in the 60's, and right about the time of Wanda Sabir's first African American Celebration of Poetry at the West Oakland (aka Huey Newton) branch of the public library, and before Youth Speaks, there was a movement to get our people together using the tools of wit and voice.

Inspired by so many great thinkers whose works have come before this —June Jordan and Poetry for the People, Ishmael Reed and *Multi-America*, KRS1 and so many, many others.

However, back then, I was not thinking about Africa. I was only thinking about Oakland. I was thinking, how can we stop black on black violence? How can we love each other again? And the wind whispered, "Sankofa." Plus, there was that movie of the same title that changed my life.

Fast forward to 2013. We now have moved fully through hip-hop and have Youth Speaks, Brave New Voices and Beyonce! We also have 3 strikes. Mass incarceration. Gentrification. Ebola. We have mass shootings and ethnic cleansing taken to new levels. Obama is president and I cannot predict the 45th. I am living in Cote d'Ivoire, and then I meet Sir Black. Sir Black has a goal to work with youth in Ghana. For him, the youth of Ghana need to stay connected to their African roots. Some are infatuated with American influences of hip-hop and rap, so, he uses the art form spoken word to teach young Ghanaians about their roots and the oral tradition. As fate would have it, I attend his first poetry slam.

I am but one person, but I had an idea. What if there was an exchange between youth in Oakland and youth in Ghana? What if the Sankofa journey could be made using technology and words? Could we host an International poetry slam in Africa? What kind of healing would then arise?

After the deaths of too many friends' sons by gun violence, I asked myself, where is my path? But, with my vision of an American Sankofa and Sir Black's commitment to African youth, could we bring healing to the world? Would these authentic returns be able to quench something within?

I believed so. And so did Sir Black. Together we spent endless hours facilitating poetic dialogue with the partner pairs. We had Skype meetings, weekly exchanges, and technology support sessions. And, when we arrived in Ghana, he was there at the airport. We arranged a beautiful program, which included the poetry slam. His team of poets accompanied us on our cultural tours and arranged our visit to Ghanatta Senior High School, where we met with students and attended a film opening.

So, this is how it began.
With desire for change.

We Are Poets

Karla Brundage

We are poets crossing the Atlantic to compete in a Poetry Slam and cultural exchange in Ghana that culminates a yearlong Pan-African poetry writing workshop. Our ages are 21-65. Our sexualities, genders, and racial identities vary. Our life experiences, socio-economic classes, and upbringings are diverse, but we are mostly Black Americans.

I am the leader of this group that has committed to writing linked poetry with exchange partners in the West African countries of Ghana and Cote d'Ivoire. We will join with Ehalakasa, our associate group that is headquartered in the city of Accra in Ghana. We will meet Sir Black and our other Ghanaian partner poets, who range from ages 18-63. Mostly, they are students at the University of Ghana, Lagon in Accra.

Finally, the day arrived. On May 15, 2018, we touched down at Accra's Kotoka International Airport to meet face-to-face the people with whom we had shared so much in the last year.

Disembarking from the plane after what felt like days, we learned to accommodate for a wheelchair and a walker—almost unheard of at the Accra airport. The heat blasted those who made it quickly through immigration. Sweat began to creep down my spine, but it was also a welcome contrast to the frigid airplane. Two of the poets had forgotten their yellow-fever cards at home. We had to pay the price in dollars and time. It suddenly hit us Americans that we were in a land where there are limits.

Three hours later, we collected our bags and headed to exchange money. Because we were a big group of Americans, the taxi drivers haggled with each other about who would take us to the hotel, all hoping for a big tip. But we had ordered a *trotro*, which was on its way. A *trotro* is similar to an American minivan. During our 30-minute wait for our vehicle, the heat swooped in, as did the mosquitoes!

People who wanted to see us better crowded in, others who wished to get past pushed on through, annoyed by the hubbub we created. We are *obroni*, which means foreigners, but has come to mean whites. As African Americans, this did not resonate, but we were blind with joy at the feeling of homecoming.

In Ghana, there is growing awareness among local people that African Americans have traceable lineage to Africa, but I heard the term "*obroni*" whispered as we walked by. It cannot be denied that our bodies held both a race and a nationality, and we carried U.S. dollars, so we created a different kind of stir. Our walks, speaking tones, and accents make us uniquely African American in the USA; ironically, these traits made us both African American and foreign in Ghana.

Suddenly, Sir Black arrived with his team: Jeneral Nta Tea and Dr. So, two comedians who bill themselves as the "2 Idiots." Their comedy act is far from idiotic. Their last production, which toured Ghana and Germany, was a re-enactment of Kafka's *The Trial* adapted to comment on the judicial and justice system in Ghana.

We were finally on our way. Ten people with 15 bags were placed into the van. And five more travelers, plus the walker, were loaded in Sir Black's 1984 model black Mercedes. Ghana! We have come here to be baptized anew!

Baptismal

Woédem Afua Parku, aka Woé, aka Z. Afua

I am waffle iron and black tea Friday nights.
I am from royal palm serenaded driveways,
high high walls, paint brushes, and
Saturday morning jazz music
I am from a Parku and Gidiglo matrimony: two extremes
of an ethnic spectrum—an unlikely pairing.
I am from a breed of women waging wars on their traumas,
Chasing demons—and a God living in their arthritic bodies
I am from deserted sea ravaged Aborlorve.
Here, where oceans bring back memories with each tide that
rolls in
From Akple and anchovies.

I am Klikor and its shrines.
I am Klikor and its church bells.
I am constricting lungs, bulimia, and chronic anxiety.
I am also father's Purple Heart
and mother's prayer beads.

I continue to rise
to remind my spirit of my resilience
To be the grace to stay.

I am from a long line of preachers and poets
of priests and orators
of linguists and storytellers.
I am from a lineage of heart disease
and Christmas dinner fights
midnight's mourn of loss
chests heaving in sorrow
shoulders leaning on against each other
hands held together in prayer
men who have neglected their women.

I am a trinket in a collection of scrap metal
anomaly of minister's touch on a baptismal lake
rippling of God's miracle
the shout out
moon for a mouth
perfect for speaking dreams into existence
wings for wrists
perfect for gathering dreams turned reality.
*From metaphors turned grenade to break traditions of
silence.*

Descended

Imani Todd

From metaphors turned grenade to break traditions of silence.
I come from Warriors land
Descended from the constellations.
4 a.m. talks with God led to my emancipation.
I'm from East Chicago nights and New Orleans mornings that
fell in love every day while San Francisco watched.

I come from brown hands and black fists—
Afro picks in my nappy hair
Catholic schools where teachers said my
Afro pick was too "political" to wear
Where the girls said my braids looked like snakes,
And when I stood up all the boys called me Sasquatch
Because I was bigger than them.
I am Medusa;
These dreadlocks will bite you if you get too close!
And you can hate this 200-pound body, but just know that I
don't.
My silhouette curves like the Oakland Hills.

My self-righteous nerve to love myself will stop
The day Cal students agree with our government.
Basically, never.

As far as I'm concerned, Steph & Ayesha Curry are my President And First Lady,
Until Barack and Michelle come back
And actually "Make America Great Again,"
Well . . . better than it used to be.

Not sure if a country founded on hate could ever be great
But, if there's one place in this state that I'm grateful to wake up in Every day,
It would be the one and only San Francisco Bay.

where i'm from

Radhiyah Ayobami

flatbush ave & fulton street
dollar cabs, black soap & sandalwood incense
sisters in flowing dresses & brothers in *kufi* calling
alafia, salaam, & peace sister how you be?

african dance classes in *kente*-cloth skirts &
summer festivals in city parks
with chain link fences

old ladies sitting on porches wide-legged
shaking their heads at young girls walking grown
with brand-new woman hips

mamas & grandmamas & aunties
living together in one house
raising children, paying bills &
cooking in big family pots

family reunions in tobacco fields &
dirt roads with no light &
sunday morning church where women in white
sit in the front pews
praying for every living thing

people that survived a treacherous crossing &
still made their lives a song flung up to heaven
cornbread & collard greens
welfare reform & the great migration
harlem renaissance & black power
straight-up old-school love.

Motherland, Ghana-Afrika

Nathaniel Ogli

Well, I wish I could say I'm
straight-up old-school love
That era when love was pure as fresh palm wine
with dew from above

Often times, my grandmother shared the tales of her love for
my grandfather

Wish I could fly back into time but I'll need a magic wand and
a grand feather

Wishes will never be horses so guess I've no choice than to
glance further

So let me tell you where I'm from

I'm from the place where fireflies trapped in bottles gave us lights

I'm from that place of wit and survival where you prove your
manhood by the number of victories recorded in fights

There were also the other boys whose victories were in the
number they "conquered" with manly might

Yeah... where your level of freedom is determined by another man's rights

Where your future is calculated before your first breath; parents' birth-rite

We leave a major part of our dreams in our mothers' wombs before we greet the earth

I grew up in a society where the elders are the stewards of wisdom
so they foretell your future right from birth

It's only when you turn 30 that you begin to live your life

The lucky ones do well to preserve their drive until that age
when they're old enough to endure a night inside the beehive

I also grew up in a society where your uncle has the family rights to spoil you

Where those who saw the sun ahead of you, give you mentoring to help you avoid a lot of what you would have had to toil through

Toddlers were allowed to eat the soil too

Now, I miss the Easter that came with hosanna and palm branches

I sure do miss the apata (house made of palm branches) where
we made merry in our Christmas with no sheets or blankets

I miss the Kweku Ananse (modern-day Spider Man) days
His double brains and cunning ways

I miss those times we lived in clay houses. Yeah . . .
It was in Christmas that we got brand new trousers

We learnt to cherish and take care of our little
Thus, every boy or girl had to keep a thread and a needle
So just incase you stretched too much, you could patch up the middle

Never will I want to trade my wakye, palm wine, fufu, banku
and okro stew

Never will I want to trade my rich culture, festivals, tourist
sites and sea view

I'll therefore smile and be grateful for where I'm from
Where our monsters were real, not Scooby Doo's Phantom

So in my next life, given the chance to choose where I want to
come from,

I'll still choose to come from the motherland, Ghana-Afrika—
this is where I am strong!!!

Agoo Hostel

Karla Brundage

Known for hosting artist groups, entrepreneurs and volunteers, Agoo Hostel is situated in the heart of Accra in Ghana. After over 24 hours of travel, we Americans were happy to be greeted by warm food, access to fresh drinking water, and a friendly and accommodating staff.

To my surprise, all the sleeping quarters were clean and well-decorated. We all had air conditioning (we expected only two rooms would have that privilege), and there was hot water for showers. Because of the flexible menu, which offered traditional as well as vegetarian and vegan meals, we all ate well. Best of all, there was Wi-Fi. During our five nights at Agoo, we were able to relax in the lounge and watch TV, or chill quietly in our rooms. We were thankful for the excellent service and the kind people we met.

After our first night, we newly arrived poets arose refreshed. Suddenly, the halls of Agoo Hostel roared with laughter. Among us new arrivals, life stories were exchanged and current politics dissected, especially the role and identities of Africans and Americans in the modern world. Who has it better? Who has it worse? Poverty, Police violence, mass incarceration, colonialism, and gender identity were among the topics we discussed with young Ghanaian and Nigerian intellectuals, and other visitors, whom we met at Agoo.

But the most significant and difficult topic was the broken connection between African Americans and Africa, the Motherland. Perceptions—what are they? Those of us whose ancestors were enslaved in the crossing of the Middle Passage now belong to the Promised Land. Descendants of slaves are now blessed with blue passports adorned with golden eagles and access to the freedom to travel. The lost and prodigal, once cast away, hope to return to open arms. Some perceive that the returnees want to reign as kings and queens.

What is this myth of the American Dream, and how will it play out in the minds of the Africans we meet? Concurrently, what is the African Dream held so dear in the minds of Black people of the diaspora, many of whom have been homeless too long? Do we shoulder the heavy burden of racism as our inheritance? Where is home?

Home

Makeda, aka Sandra Hooper Mayfield

Home

I went Home

Home to people who love me, just because I belong to them
Home to roots and seven living generations
To trees that hold family secrets and paths worn bare from the
      coming and going of the nine generations
Home where Papa Earl's shotgun is behind the door
   and the courting table he made, which serves the ninth
   generation

Home to where the Great Aunts built upon the foundation he
    laid for our future
Home to sienna-colored men and sometimes toothless women
    who stay, till death do they part
Home to laughter, and food and love that feeds the mind body and
    spirit
Home to women who sit on the porch in their slips and tell
    stories
    bout the old days and kin folks called Suga Du
Home to the spot where they hung Uncle Brady when he was
    only nine years old

Home to James Edward, Tony, and Sheila—and Cousin Blu,
		who calls me double
	cuz slavery taught us painful things
Home to a church in the clearing, holding the lifted-up voices
		of my ancestors
Home where we laid Aunt Clara, the heartbeat of the family,
		to rest

I went Home

Home to Remember

Etchian Jean Frédéric Orbeli

I went Home to remember who I was.

Through my paths on those crooked ways
      and across the plain
I can smell the particular scent of the sweating plants
      and the soil pummeled by the sun and the rain
Through the wild landscapes hiding physical and spiritual
      creatures with fierce muzzles, paws, and claws.

My paths I tread with uncertainty lead to my grandfather's
      cocoa plantation
Where I hope to find answers about who I am from where
      I come.

I wish this old man, faithful heir of my ancestors' legacy
      will help me find out where my fears arise
      why being far from my home makes me experience so
      much alienation.

"My home is big, old, and pleasant," he said,
"Home of proud Men, pure rivers, sacred forests, and
      legendary hosts.

Beautiful haven protected by its fierce soldiers and the spirits
of its ghosts."

His home is big, old, and pleasant, as he said, and now that I
can finally say so,
I see! I don't need to know that much to feel its sweet warmth.

Now that I have come in, and am able to feel the joy of it, it is
surely worth all of it!

Fat Tuesday

Makeda, aka Sandra Hooper Mayfield

We went to Nana house for
Catholic Friday fish and fries,
coleslaw, pound cake
scrumptious, icebox lemon pies.
But my favorite day was Tuesday
when those who were able
could hear my Daddy making love
to Mama at the dining table.
He made love creative like
fairy tales and fables to describe
how good Mama's food was
to those who sat around the table.
Visitors would smile and blush
even Auntie Mable,
when they heard my Daddy making love
to my Mama at the table.
Oh, Daddy was dramatic
mmmm, ohhh, baby, this is good
he moaned and crooned
for breakfast lunch and dinner
and as often as he could.
Mama was blushing red,
like beans and rice, Daddy's favorite.
"Pass the cornbread honey and the hot sauce,"

then he would kiss her sweetly on her cheek,
not just once but twice.
Many years have gone by since I sat at that table.
Now I don't believe in fairy tales and fables,
but I would do anything if just one more time
I was able to hear my Daddy making love to
Mama at the table.

Fufu and Palm Nut Soup

Etchian Jean Frédéric Orbeli

With **Mama at the table**, all the plates are served full.

Her red palm nut soup with the
yellow pounded *fufu*
full of crabs, beef skin,
dried fish,
meat of grasscutter from the bush
leaves us speechless.

Perhaps the old cooking pot contains
the secret of her talent
or maybe the wood fire burning inside the stove
she made from the finest clay.

But when we see the rainbow in her eyes
watching us silent
we can deeply feel
that it is all about the love she puts into her soup
every day, night and day
because true love has a unique flavor.

Left Top to Bottom to Right Top to Bottom

1. The first handcrafted book of poetry helped to establish WO2WA's work in the community.
2. Artist activists like Donte Clark helped promote WO2WA.
3. Local establishments such as The Back Room allowed the group to use their venue for fundraising.
4. From West Oakland Library to the Oakland Library, poets shared their work with the community at public events.
5. Karla, Shoshanna. Adeshima, Zakkiyah, Xiomara, Mimi, Rucha, Sara, Tyrice and Wanda pose at a speakeasy inspired fundraising event.

3

The Poets Meet

Karla Brundage

This was the day we had all been waiting for. After a good night's rest at Agoo Hostel, we arose refreshed. We gathered for our first writing activity.

Sir Black arrived at Agoo Hostel, and we decided to meet the poets from Ehalakasa at the W.E.B. DuBois Pan African Cultural Center, but realized that transportation for over twenty people would cost too much money in taxi fare. Finally, we decided that all of the Ghanaian poets would come to Agoo Hostel, which had been the original plan.

Although our original exchange group consisted of fifteen people that participated in the written poetry exchange, ten American poets were able to make the trip to Ghana. Of the ten, we were nine African Americans and one Jewish American who identifies as white. Also, two more poets—one from Cote d'Ivoire and one from the U.S.—would join us the next day.

The poets entered one by one, and met their partners for the first time. The room began to fill with laughter, and hugs were exchanged as American counterparts greeted the person with whom they had been exchanging letters for close to a year. Because of social media, we had seen photos and even videos of each other as well as exchanged greetings and poetry via Skype while sitting in my living room.

However, there is nothing like physical connections, the ability to make contact, embrace and look someone in the eye. Sharing space is such an intimate act.

In the U.S. right now, the idea of space is so alive: we have safe spaces and free speech spaces and makers-space, but a lot of our exchanges seem to be through technological spaces. This is why it was invigorating for us to have our black and white bodies connect with, and touch other black bodies. This moment felt as if the goal of the exchange had already been achieved, but it was only the beginning.

In circle, we shared our names, one thing we loved and—as in the African tradition—shared about the health and welfare of our families, as well as our place in the family tree. The introductions went sort of like this. *I am Karla, I love poetry. I have one sister and a daughter. I am the oldest in my family. I am a teacher of English and the leader of this group. I am so happy to be here.*

As each person shared their story, we learned who was in the room. We were students, teachers, poets, aspiring filmmakers, musicians, comedians, retired folks, a newly married couple, and three grandmothers.

We received a warm welcome.

Unity

Xiomara

I am we
a piece of the whole
the collective essence of life.

We are the roar of the sea
smashing against the cliffside
or the salt left behind in the grains of sand
sweet sugar mango glowing
as it drops into eager hands
mouths hungry for its nectar
the sun beating down on a dirt road
while heat waves dance in the distance
the earth that quakes in summer time
or the pulse of once-still waters.

Winds of Time
of times past
excite the surface.

I am we
a piece of a whole
the collective essence of life
thriving in the embrace of our mothers' arms
backs strong as ancient bedrock
her hair wild like the mangroves of old.

Wild

Nathaniel Ogli

Her hair wild like the mangroves of old
take a seat, relax and watch the story unfold.
This is the story of a black folk untold.

Just like the mangroves, let my existence sink into
the hemisphere of your mind where your "son" grows.

See my name written in the amber
anytime the sun glows.
Lemme be that first sound you hear
anytime the cock crows.

Cos like the stream of water that flows
into a river source where no man knows
only the father knoweth where the son goes.

But in all my splendor and array.
I need that white in order to form gray.

Therefore, there's no me if there's no we.
I need you to attain the height of "glowry" (glory).
Fit into my puzzle and be my clue

when I'm lost in the maze.
Be my key when I'm locked in the cage.
Be the mask that hides the ugliness in my face.
You're my complementing calm nature
anytime the demons switch me up into the mode of rage.

So please clean up my scar.
I am because you are.
I'll survive on land only because you're a star.

Ascendencia

Xiomara

I'll survive on land only because you're a star
A child of Her
The Queen of the Night
Mi Mama Primera
Our First Mother.

She hangs in the sky and visits me every night.
Her shining face cools the warm seas
And heals tender skin.

Our melanin is burned by the sun
Rejected by a concept of light and dark
Chained to the ground like animals they've created in their
blind brilliance.
Kingdom stretches across the Earth
Blooming in the hidden spaces of a universe
divided and conquered.

Her body is a marvel of the cosmos
Her crown made up of constellations in the sky.
She is the pull in the waves
As they crash on the shore at twilight.
She is the dew that drops from the heavens
Feeding dead grass of yesterday.

She is the howl of a storm
And sweet caress of a midnight wind.
She lulls me to sleep and mends my spirit

So as I'm trapped here on land
The unforgiving inferno of the sun beating on my back
I remind myself of you, your eyes.
I see God in you,
And She is beautiful

Beauty

Nathaniel Ogli

And She is beautiful.
Her beauty compares to none.

No parish priest can overcome the temptation
of looking at her twice, even when she becomes a nun.
Believe me when I say,
She carries with her the radiance of the sun.

Providing shelter for others
her eyes glow with magnificence.

Some call her arrogant when to no avail
they try to fathom her intelligence.
Providing shelter for the other elements,
she is the protector of the realms and god of defense.

Sophisticated in nature
the finest creature ever made by "Oboade" the Creator,
she knows what she's made of.
Her uniqueness defines her;

Perfect model for her daughters and sons
she lays out the structure for tribes and clans.
Her name is Culture, the delight of her loved ones.

On Meeting Wild-Flower

Crystal Tettey

Poetry Exchange, "West Oakland to West Africa" (WO2WA), gave the meadows of Accra, Ghana, Wild-Flower in May 2018. Writing with my Exchange Partner was effortless! We were one in thought, in trauma, in heritage, in Hope.

Conversations with Wild-Flower unlocked the doors to centuries of shared experiences. We wrote as we spoke. We let our Hearts lead and edited little, eager to preserve the rawness of our feelings.

Both dedicated to painting trans-generational Hope, we paid homage to our shared Forbearers:

shipped Me
worked Me
murdered Me
and never returned Me

cut off from my lineage
given a name unpronounceable
asked to be thankful for my new "home"

Together, we dreamed of a brighter trans-Atlantic future . . .

Inferior

Crystal Tettey, Refrain by Wild-Flower

The label is "inferior"
    "uncivilized"
    for one imperfect in the master's language

shipped Me
worked Me
murdered Me
and never returned Me

I learnt Poetry in neither Mother nor Father tongue
What would Edgar Allan Poe make of this tragedy?
cursed to express emotions that do not inhabit me

words closest in meaning
not nearly a match for my thoughts

shipped Me
worked Me
murdered Me
and never returned Me

cut off from my Lineage

given a name unpronounceable
asked to be thankful for my new "home"

shipped Me
worked Me
murdered Me
and never returned Me

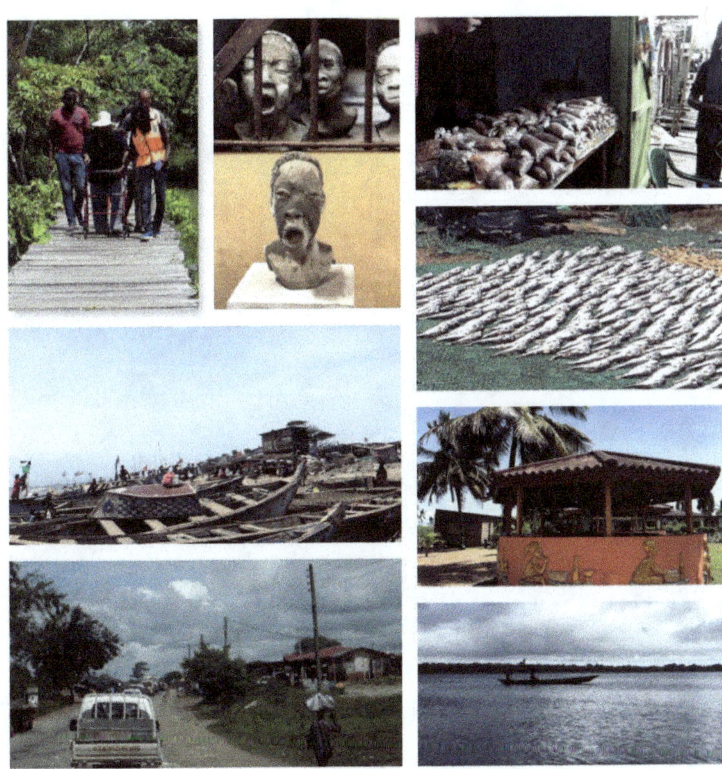

1. The Ghanaian community respects their elders. Mama Makeda was everyone's mother, she was showered with love and support as the poets traveled across the country.
2. Clay replicas in the Cape Coast Dungeons served as physical reminders of what it felt like to be stolen from land.
3. A local herbal store at the Nzulu Village.
4. Boats line the shore in Apam, Ghana and transported the poets to the Haduwa Arts and Culture Center where the winning palm seed was planted.
5. Fresh fish was the delicacy most poets chose to eat during their visit.
6. The scenery between locations was filled with vivid images of Ghanaian daily life.
7. Alberta's Place in Cape Coast had some the best fish and beaches.
8. The women of the Nzulu Village community are seen here boating to the main land.

5

Meeting Prince Joey

Zakiyyah G. E. Capehart

The West African poets were coming to visit the West Oakland poets at the hostel where we were staying. We, the West Oakland poets were all busy preparing for their arrival. However, we didn't know if they would actually make it, because it was raining so hard. I had never experienced rain of that magnitude. It was as if billions of buckets of water were being poured simultaneously from the sky. There was also a lot of flooding taking place in Accra that day as well. But we didn't realize that the Ghanaians were used to this heavy rainy season and all the flooding it brought. Then just as our West African poet partners had promised, they showed up.

The day we all finally met was most joyous! I met my Ghanaian poet partner—Prince Joey. We were excitedly embracing and hugging each other. It reminded me of the family reunions I experienced with my biological family. Prince Joey and I were both very happy to meet in person. We had already met on the Internet. Our groups had shared poetry on Skype. And he and I had been writing poems to each other for approximately a year.

The two of us embraced and hugged for a long while. He is my grandson's age; therefore, it felt like I was meeting another grandson for the first time. We held on to one another as if we'd lose each other, if we let go. Standing up, we talked a long time. Then we sat down beside each other and continued to chat.

Prince Joey is one of six sons in his family. He and his twin brother are the youngest of the siblings. He is a 21-year-old college student employed at a restaurant. Other than being a poet, Prince Joey is also a filmmaker and actor.

During our conversation he told me about the film he made with a couple of his friends. Emmanuel Akambo is also a poet member of the group. He said the film was to premiere that weekend. I was very excited to be in Ghana during his film viewing, so I asked him to announce his film to the group. So, we adjusted our schedule so we could attend. The film was an interesting comedy, and we laughed a lot. It was shown outdoors on an enchanting Ghana evening, in an intimate garden setting. I enjoyed witnessing another aspect of my poet partner's creativity. Prince Joey is a respectful, conscious Ghanaian young man. I'm glad we were chosen to be poet partners, to build fires in our writing.

Fires in Oakland

Zakiyyah G. E. Capehart

we always get screwed and that's the drill
the West Oakland apartment building fire
was not on the news
when i heard about it
i got the blues
it touched my heart
and ripped it apart
a tragic fire blazing in the night
causing unimaginable fright
most were asleep
but began to weep

fire burning
smoke filling eyes, clogging throats
babies crying, children screaming
afraid   disoriented   confused
one hundred black people displaced
because of a landlord's greed
property owners, speculators, developers too
all conspiring against me and you

does anybody care?

fire took the lives
of people who lived there
multiple violations, building rundown, holes in walls
ceilings threatening to fall
water leaks causing mold
electrical wires exposed
pipes rusted filled with lead
a drink of water could kill you dead
rats, roaches, bedbugs, running amuck
but the landlord still wants his buck

one hundred black people displaced
driven into the street
no shelter, no clothing, no water, no food
the ghost ship fire
was all over the news
are the deaths and displacement
of black people unimportant news?

elders   disabled people   families with children

those who survived are homeless now

Floods in Ghana

Joseph Atsu Korgan, aka Wordrite

Those who survived are homeless now—
Out in the open people rushed home lest they get wet.

As electricity sliced across the night sky, thunder rumbled
Warning souls marked in Death's register.
Lightning struck several with a formless flash
As if taking photographs for the obituary
Of those cleared away like trash.

Farmers smiled ear to ear
Their long-awaited wish for real rain was here—
It was June!

The sky deepened about to pour bitumen.
Heaven wore a pitch-black suit
Like it was already mourning unknown souls.

When the ice melted
The sky wept bitterly onto earth
Whether tears of joy or of sorrow.

Who knew it would bring us pain tomorrow?

Water won the race on earth,
Like Usain Bolt on a marathon row.

The water ran and ran
Dragging property, dragging souls
Along with it
Moving cars against their will
Attacking buildings that owe no bill
Sometimes considerate enough to go through the drains
But pushed back onto the streets by garbage
Carelessly dumped in there by humans considered sane.
On one part of the earth there was a war
A tag-team wrestling match
The downpour teaming up with fuel and electricity
Strong enough to bring down property and humanity.

In one cool part of the capital city
Mankind didn't stand a chance.
The rest of the story proves
Our lives aren't in our own hands.

At the end of it all
Nature won the tug of war.
The angel of death got more companions than it needed
In a day.

Greeted by a Rainbow

Zakiyyah G. E. Capehart

I come from a place
where greeting is paramount
a place where the moon
appears full each night
a place where the darkness
highlights zillions of stars
that kiss the sky
and brighten our path
through thickness in the woods
at the midnight hour
a place where the doors
are never locked
even as you sleep
a place where dew-drops halt
on the first note
the songbird sings
a place where porch swings
sing a lullaby to passersby
a place where summer breezes
soothe your sneezes

a place where neighbors talk
and children walk to play
in the early morning sun
greeted by a rainbow
I come from a place where
sunlight moonlight and starlight
is etched on the faces of the people

and shone throughout the universe
I come from a place where
pyramids are erected
at the enfolds of the
cerebrum cerebellum and medulla
I come from a place where
experiencing bitter hot sour and sweet

are precursors to life's journey
I come from a place where
greeting is a way of life
it begins and never ends

Beats of Difference

Joseph Atsu Korgan, aka Wordrite

It begins and never ends
The streets, the star-less sky, the people
The feet beating the beats of difference on the ground,
The wolves in sheepskin . . .
It begins and never ends.
Their actions blinded by the palms of their ego,
Those are my people.
We live in the same neighborhood, but we're unequal.
Some work hard to make certain some of us believe so.
No neighbor's mood is really the worry of another.
There are many women,
but the only one you truly have is your mother.
Some homes are wet enough with tears,
But they appear vulnerable enough to break easily
As if they've been rather dry for years.
Yet there's the morning sunshine
The light that brings the day into full view,
The day that reminds us that
there are a lot of blessings in a queue.
The scorching sun melts away our worry
That keeps our eyes wide open
during the darkness in the night.

The aroma of groundnut, palm, or *okro* soup
That we sniff makes us feel more hyper than the effect of coke.
We're inspired to see the worries as a joke.
Jukeboxes from distant pubs and shops bring a rhythmic background to our thoughts.
The kids across the streets bring the river above our feet,
But we hope not to drown in the memory of our childhood.
We share with them what we have, so they won't grow up and know us for what we know the elders for.
The clean teeth they show us tell us that a lot has changed.
So those who have done it wrong all this while,
Pulling strings to make things work all in their interest,
Will know sooner than they realize
That the guitar will be taken away.

Accra Historical Tour: Jamestown

Karla Brundage

We went on a historical tour of Accra's district called Jamestown, a remnant name from colonial times. Traditionally, the district is known as Gamashie. On this day, it was 30 degrees C, or 86 degrees Fahrenheit. Those of us who needed more time to get ready delayed the communal breakfast. After a rushed meal, we were finally ready to board the bus. But we did not know where we want to go first.

Jamestown was overwhelming. There, unlike Agoo Hostel, I experienced the fatigue that comes from privilege. The poverty was overwhelming. People welcomed us into their homes, and we saw how they live.

Most of the residents occupied brick housing units connected in rows, haphazard in appearance, as if they could be melted back into the sand by a big rain.

Women sat outside their homes fanning themselves to dissuade the heat and flies. Children followed our group, hoping for candy.

Despite the poverty, I imagined myself sitting under an umbrella, my head wrapped, legs wide, fanning the heat from under my skirt. I would call out to women carrying water from an imagined well, my children playing at my feet, or running freely through the streets.

That could be my Black life.

My Black Life

Wanda Sabir

Black life.

Pray for me, I ask silently to

the surgeons robed in white

pointy hats within.

Perhaps their god

will have mercy on their souls

since I have none.

Thumb out, my heart—

freed from its container at 11:56 p.m. (4/20);

then again 10:33 p.m. and 7:20 p.m. (4/22);

and 11: 05 pm (4/27)]

reaches out to the kitty floating by.

Can I join you? I ask.

    I wait for an answer.

I Lost You

Mariska Araba Taylor-Darko

I wait for an answer
Not from you but from God,

Your body was brought to me
Wrapped in a white shroud,
The scars and scratches still raw
As though you had been struck with a claw.

That was the day my heart died.

On my knees I screamed to God,

Pain wracked my body
As I clung to my own self.

Arms wrapped around me
Rocking me tenderly.

"Why oh why?" I cried out to God.

"Give me an answer, do you not know everything?"

I lost you just like that.

Now, I wander around like a lost soul searching for my love.

A Freed Woman

Wanda Sabir

He lived in the syllables
Between particles of sand stuck to my toes.

Now, I wander around like a lost soul searching for my love.

Better forgotten.

Waterfall drenched
No room for
Any others.

We fit perfectly,
Until I slipped
Off the rock.

Tumbling,
There was no one to catch me.
Pain is all I remember;
When I think about it.

An Old African Dances Inside What Remains[1]

Wanda Sabir

I never told you before
but I love all things purple and sweet:
Berries
Juices
African violets
Ceremonial Robes
Osumare[2] particles spilling into pots of gold

I avoid heat –

    heated irons pots forks letters foreign names family
seals; *Sweet Jesus's* dropped anchor & later bon voyage
Coal stoves
Fire pits
Hell
Standing stirring sitting shackled contemplating – stowaways
Stowing away in decks below . . . on islands made of pristine
bones, polished like silver, Shangó's lightning flash . . . Oya's[3]
winds, Shangó's thunderclaps
Jumping
Swimming away

Water does not support fire, an element ancestors have learned
to do without (on the ocean floor)
—in the deep deep waters
Olókun's[4] realm
(Soul survival a compromise)

This inherited trauma
Unspeakable yet alive
Keeps me trapped on land where I avoid
heated soups
fried melons
boiled yams

Capsized in a West Oakland field
My basket magically fills with kale and okra
zucchini, pumpkins
walnuts and sage
Reclining on spinach pilaf pillows

I lie in the edible garden as *Birds of Paradise* flutter about . . .
Oshun[5] a sticky pollination
The choir is rehearsing for a concert I dare not miss
Ruby-throated Hummingbirds are singing in the alcoves—
theirs a rich gospel rumble
(While) Belted Kingfishers play percussion
The soloist is of course the Black-capped Chickadee—her
laugher as welcome as her impossibly high notes

Invited guests include the *Twittering Quartet* with Mourning Dove, Great Blue Heron, Baltimore Oriole, and Eastern Bluebird; Blue Jay is a favorite for her cool outtakes; the legacy biddies: Northern Cardinal and American Robin round out the program.

I call it – *Spirit-fare*, eat and be merry—

table set

for *life* & *after that*.

---

[1]_*The Old African* (2005), a children's book by Julius Lester, illustrated by Jerry Pinkney.

[2] Osumare —orisha or Black deity that governs the rainbow

[3] Óya and Shango were a couple at one point. Óya is the guardian or change and transformation. She guards the cemeteries and is the strong wind; hurricanes and tropical storms. She does not forget her children snatched, stolen and sold in West Africa where the storms originate each year and pummel the southern shores of America where her children landed aboard slave ships. Shango is the warrior king whose voice is heard in the thunder, face seen in the lightning. He is one of the warrior *orisha* which includes: Elégbá, Ògún and Òshoosì.

[4] Olókun is *orisha* of the deep deep waters, what August Wilson, playwright's_Aunt Ester called *Land of the Bones*.

[5] Oshun -- Goddess of Love. I evoke Oshun as *eros*— pollination, an erotic physical manifestation of love for *plants*, for *speaker*.

Culture

Mariska Araba Taylor-Darko

I'm missing you.

That day you died, I shouted but could not even cry.
The family swarmed around like bees instructing me what to do.

Because I now wore the clothes of widowhood, they said:
"A widow must not speak."

"Why?" I asked.

"It is tradition."
"It is our culture."
"You must be silent when people are around."
"Being chatty makes people think you are enjoying
the attention."
"So you must be quiet."

Even in grief they want to control me
Control my emotions, control my tears
In the name of culture.

Now the years have gone by

And I finally met an elder who explained,

"Long ago there were no therapists or counselors
Like we have now. The only way for you to keep your sanity
was to be silent and watch what was going on around you."

The wise one added,

"But if you began chatting day and night
After all the mourners had left
And you were alone
You would continue chatting to yourself
And end up doing it without knowing it."

Sometimes, it is wise to listen to the elders.
For every act called culture
Has a reason for existing.
We just have to search for the reason.

1. WO2WA poets visited Ghanatta Senior High where scholars shared their work and asked questions about written verses spoken word.
2. Tyrice and two Ghanatta students shared their love for Rihanna breaking out into a dance circle after this picture.
3. Wanda Sabir takes a moment to gaze over the Atlantic, in remembrance and peace for the then and now.
4. *Do you have games on your phone?* Imani and Xiomara sharing screen time with a young boy from Old Cape Coast, Jamestown.
5. Mariska, Nathaniel, Akambo, and Jewell-King Speaks four of Ehalakasa's most moving wordsmith share space at Agoo Hostel.

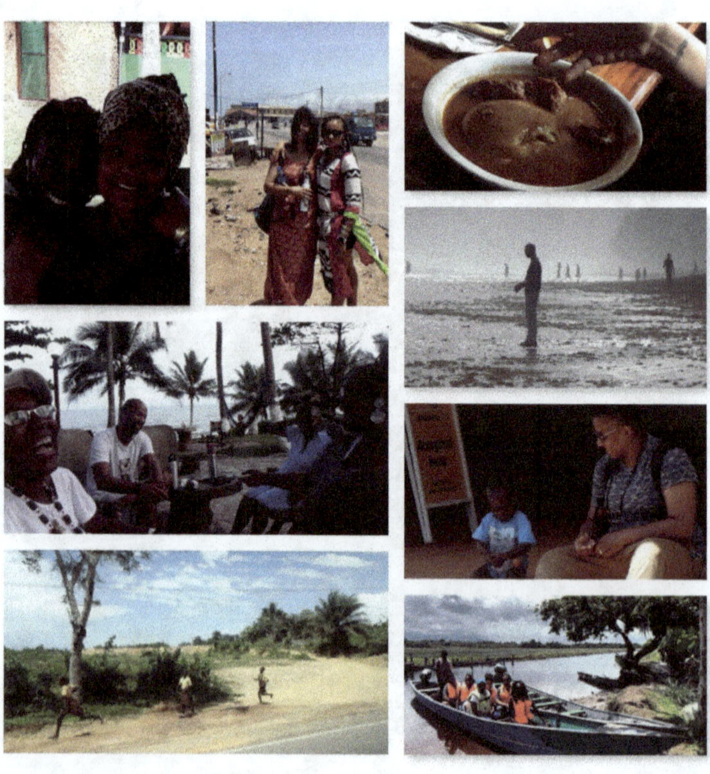

Left to Right

1. Makeda and her poet partner Obi became family long before physical contact.
2. Karla and Tyrice stand in Old Accra also known as Jamestown.
3. Tyrice quickly learned the etiquette of home.
4. Sister Imakus, Adeishma, Zakiyyah, and Mama Makeda share a laugh on Cape Coast beach at One Africa. Owner, Sister Imakus, created a space for reflection and peace.
5. Adeshima looks across the Atlantic honoring Sankofa.
6. Young female scholars in Dodowa run with freedom.
7. Wild-Flower shares a moment playing the Kashaka with a child before the boat ride to Nzulu Village.
8. Poets; Obi, Zakiyyah, Imani, Wild-Flower, Tyrice (and spouse) headed to Nzulu Village to meet the community.

7

The W. E. B. Du Bois Center

Karla Brundage

On our first full day, some of us were privileged to visit the W. E. B. Du Bois Center. At the behest of Ghana's first president after Independence, Du Bois moved to Ghana at the end of his life and collaborated with Kwame Nkrumah. Nkrumah had been an organizer of the first Pan-African National Congress in 1945. This congress is known to have been a key factor in the liberation of many African countries from colonialism, including Ghana, which gained independence in 1957. In 1961 Nkrumah invited Dr. Du Bois to Ghana to take charge of the *Encyclopedia Africana* project.

Du Bois lived in Accra with his second wife, Nina Gomer Du Bois, until her death. While there, he worked with Nkrumah and completed several books on African and African American history and liberation. Du Bois also died in Accra in

1963. He and his wife are buried in a beautiful mausoleum near his last home, which has been converted into the museum and center. This was our first stop on our journey. The connection between Africa and America cannot be any more apparent when examining the collaboration of these two great freedom fighters and intellectual thinkers.

Formerly, Ghana was a colony of Britain from 1867 until achieving its independence in 1957. As a result of its association with the U.K., Ghana has longstanding ties with the United States. Ghana has also maintained relationships with other European nations including France and Germany.

Today, the Alliance Francaise (France) and the Goethe Center (Germany) encourage artistic and literary expression in Ghana and other African nations. GROUP'S China has also supported arts and culture in Ghana.

Although U.S. foundations have shown little interest in arts and culture endeavors in Ghana, WO2WA was surprised and encouraged to be warmly welcomed both by our community-based partners and by the U.S. Embassy.

At the end of the day we taxied back to the Agoo Hostel, where we had dinner. That night, jet lag hit hard.

Mother's Wisdom

Marcus Lorenzo Penn, aka Adeshima

I went home tired and weary
And needed my mother to be near me.

I was working so hard my eyes were teary.
My mind was spent, my outlook dreary.

My mother gave me a big hug and sat me down.
Her intuition knew what was behind my frown.

She said, "Precious, I know you need rest from learning.
And to rest on the road does not end your journey."

This wisdom rippled through me like a stone in a pond.
Through all these years many times I've called upon.

That moment I laid my head on my mother's chest
To collect myself for a time of rest.

Her wisdom has proven fruitful overtime
When my life has shown up less than sublime.

Just Come and See

Emmanuel Akambo

When my life has shown up less than sublime
Unlike Marcus I then fail to rhyme
Because on the streets are boards without sign
Destiny is a celebrity taking my predicaments and sign
When speechless just mime

Just come and see
Telling you about my land style
Boasting about our achievement file
How Michael Jackson couldn't moonwalk one mile
For Beyoncé's secret my number you dial

Just come and see
My local girls have curves
That will make Oakland boys lose their nerves
Fertility itself preserves
They handle guys well knowing a good meal they deserve
Before true love other drivers they deprive
Like good manners to maintain virginity they strive

Just come and see
That I have a crush on honey
So I fell in love with a bee

On the sea I see
My mystery self using blade to cut a tree
Like jungle birds my enemies flee

The story goes on
PG 18 is not always porn
Different places we were born
Wrong teachings cause I brains to be torn
But I tell you if you want to know the truth
About someone or a place
Just come and see

Death Stole Her

Marcus Lorenzo Penn, aka Adeshima

Death stole her before 8 a.m. with two sons by her side
I never told you this but one of them heard her last sigh
In that moment he was blind and lost his sight
In an instant he was in a flashback bouncing on her thigh
At that moment of her death he did ask God why
But he knew she was going up to a place high in the sky
The day before family and friends all came by
To pay their last respects and to say goodbye
They could tell her last moments on Earth were nigh
These last moments spent were sweet like apple pie
Each of the immediate family got to spend a night
Connecting with her and hoping they might
Say all the things that they wanted to that night
About all the good and things that brought her light
The family took turns touching her skin soft not tight
They knew death was near but tried not to feel fright
At any moment the spirit of death very well might
Take a whole lot more than just her sight
It would take her entire life
And with gratitude they knew she no longer had to fight
And her only job was to walk towards the light

Towards the Light

Emmanuel Akambo

And her only job was to walk towards the light
She always told her son time will tell
In time the world will hear like a Christian church bell
Like a global village you don't need a market to buy or sell
Misfortune is marrying a woman with the mind of a girl

He complained, we are poor
Our Poverty is like a chronic sore
Even miracles couldn't get to their Poverty's core
Nor uproot its roots from life's floor
Mother still said time will tell

He complains
My mates look better
Their girls prettier
Travel further
Mother still said time will tell
He always stares at the clock
He prays to God not to be a son but at least his flock
The good Shepherd is always on his blog

Mother's time wasn't on watch but calendar

For before her son, she was a car lender
Created an investment account for her son
Which was inspired by her husband then a bartender

As all hopes seemed fading away
On his 20th birthday, a call from the bank
The boy now goes to mom's grave to grieve
For mom knew on his 20th birthday he'd be a billionaire
But before his 20th birthday was his trial to know Poverty
To enable him to appreciate property

Our mom is God

Stepping into my Elderhood at the Enslavement Dungeons

Zakiyyah G. E. Capehart

We visited the Enslavement Dungeons today. It was heart-wrenching to see where our ancestors were held captive right in Ghana. Europeans built the Enslavement Dungeons that they called "Castles," right on the coast in Cape Coast and Elmina.

Our ancestors were chained, shackled and locked in extremely small, dark, damp, cold dungeons. No light entered from the outside, except through a tiny hole leveled with the ground. Hundreds of Africans were packed on top of one another in a hole disguised as a room. They ate, defecated, and slept in that space. They did not receive any sunshine, adequate air, or exercise. Then after months in the dungeons, they were thrown into the bowels of a ship sailing to a new country.

I walked around the tiny space looking at the inhumane rock-hard walls, floor and ceiling, where hundreds of our ancestors were caged. There were only ten of us in our group, and we barely had enough space to move around in the Dungeons. My eyes swelled with water, but the shock prevented my tears from falling.

The ancestors were present with us in spirit. We visited with their spirits, and shared the food we brought to feed them. We prayed and meditated calling out their names, during the libation ceremony.

Sistah Imahkus, our guide asked for the eldest in the group, to step forward and give homage to our ancestors. I stepped forward because I was the eldest. I didn't know I would be called upon to speak. I had no idea what to say. But the words came and flowed effortlessly from my mouth. Honoring our ancestors was a spiritual epitome for me. It was an auspicious moment in time. I was very blessed and very thankful to have the privilege and the freedom.

Freedom

Tamaris Usher

If this is what freedom means, then I'll be a slave to the culture because being a slave to you is cancerous. You used to get me high like three grams of cannabis. Now I don't want to see you because you stomped on my heart. So many things I want to say to you, I don't know where to start. Sometimes, I miss you; other times, I can't stand the sight of you. I don't know how I feel about you. I'm not going to lie to you. You belittled me, and my heart took a hell of a beating. The only friends I have now are my inner demons. Because you made me emotionless, I hate the way love feels, blood full of iron and my heart is now made of steel. ***Sometimes you can't get WHO you want in life. You either LOVE it or HATE it. Just embrace the MONSTER that you created.***

Monster

Dodzi Korsi Aveh, aka WhoIsDeydzi

Sometimes you can't get WHO you want in life. You either LOVE it or HATE it. Just embrace the MONSTER that you created. If I knew this early on, I'd never had approached you. You looked all perfect before I came. Well, you still are, just that now I'm hurting. I remember your smile. Well, it used to light up my world, my very sun, and I thought my son would have it too. Now all I see is a full moon reminding me that I'm a fool, and my demons will hunt me soon. I thought you were my everything. Well, love is blind. I wished I had one eye, so in the Nick of time I'll patch things up before the Fury rose in seeking some Avengers. I thought I could mold you to suit me. I molded me to suit you. Blind, I was a reverse Pygmalion. Well, I created a beast within. To be frank, I'm the only Dr. Who that can cure this illness eating me from the intestines. Love failed the tests. Dammit Dr. Frankenstein. Our love was supposed to be indestructible. I was usually the Striker, you now my Ex, the weapon that's now hunting me, Weapon X. Well I'm supposed to be alright, but what good is a healing factor if its cancer eating you up from a clawed heart? So I carry my Bruces up like a Banner, cos I'm unashamed of the monster within. I just might go green. Hulk out and heal. Green. Regrowth. Regenerate. We just might wade in between Will&Sin. Well that's how life is. We're mostly swimming in a Deadpool. So when you see me in the corner of my web sulking, note that I'm no longer your Kweku Ananse, I lost my love, now a Black Widow. Poisonous. Trapped in your web of lies. ***Love is a fairy tale, happily never after. Screw fairytales. I'm in for comic relief.***

Love

Tamaris Usher

Love is a fairy tale, happily never after. Screw fairytales. I'm in for comic relief. Bury my face in comic books because I don't want to look at nothing else. You leave this world in a hearse. I wish I was a daredevil playing the devil's advocate in a church. I don't want to see your face because I feel betrayed. I wish I never saw what I seen. My blood has turned cold. I can feel it in my stream. I wish you didn't see how I felt about you because now I feel weak. I wish I couldn't see the agony of defeat. I wish darkness consumed my pupils. That way, I couldn't see this fucked up earth. I'm kind of glad I can't see myself with you because I might get hurt. We are nothing but trouble, the modern-day Bonnie & Clyde. Sometimes, you support my thoughts of suicide. Our relationship is complex. That's why I keep it concealed under my bed, regardless if you're in my life. You might keep me ALIVE, or I might end up DEAD. I keep my distance. My memories of you are a blur and tucked. If I'm not there to do it, someone else might pick you up. ***But seeing is believing, and my perspective will always change. What's better going blind? Or going insane?***

Seeing Is Believing

Dodzi Korsi Aveh, aka WhoIsDeydzi

But seeing is believing, and my perspective will always change. What's better going blind? Or going insane?

I don't really know. Where I come from actions speak louder than words. If you are blind, you wouldn't know crap. That's insanity. And maybe that's the problem with us. We know too much. We see differences, and frankly speaking, the world would be better if we saw less. We would know no race or color, just people. Ever since man bit that first apple, we've been seeing things we're not supposed to. We paint the rest of it on the back of our iPhones. We envied Steve's Job, thinking it had the keys to Bill's Gate which wasn't really locked hair, nor Afro. Take off that screensaver. Open your eyes. Their windows to the soul, take a deep breathe with your eyes—and, if you're still too blind to read in between, you'll realize you're empty. Something's been eating you up from the inside. Cancer, call the chemotherapist. Your horoscope couldn't predict this cancer. Maybe the darkness ain't such a bad thing. The darker the berry, the sweeter the juice. The only light we get around here is a coke light, and maybe if we were actually really blind, we'd actually see the wrong we've done. Insanity is when one's reason extends beyond the reality of the world. Ask Tiresias, who fears if everyone is wondering if he's worthy. It's prob'ly just a stone on my forehead and not my third eye. You can take it to Infiniti and back. My view would remain the same. Only the blind can see the bigger picture. Well, it's writing in Braille and read by the heart.

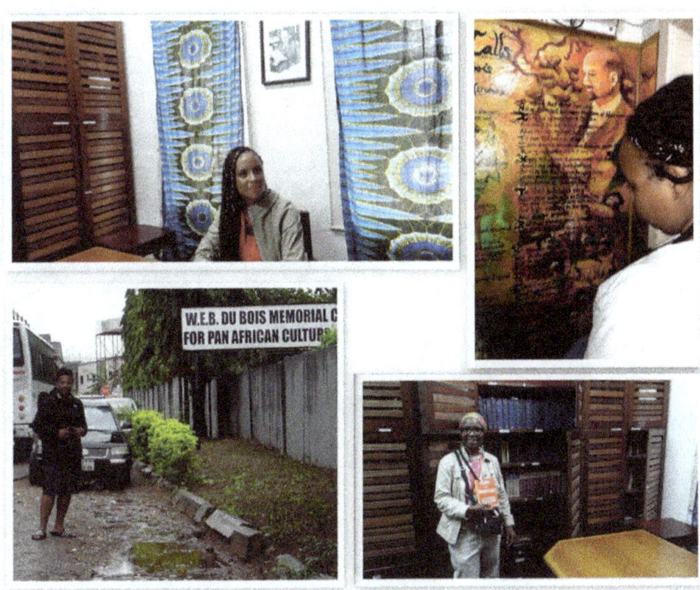

Left to Right

1. Tyrice sits in the library of African American thinker and scholar, W.E.B. Du Bois, respecting the sacred study of such a remarkable man.
2. Xiomara reads a poem that is scribed on the wall inside Du Bois' home.
3. The Pan- African movement's goal to unify those of the African diaspora inspired WO2WA: here Wild-flower pays homage.
4. Wanda stands before the books both written and studied by the great W.E.B. Du Bois

9

The Door I Never Exited

Tyrice Deane Brown

Crouched down in front of a shrine of offerings, with my knees pressing into the dirt floor of the Female Dungeon, I sense a flood of history cascade over my body. I am remembering, feeling, something that I cannot explain in English. Praying is the closest word I find to describe my actions. Not to a God do I pray, but to the spirits that hold me there long after the rest of the travelers have left, already stepping out of the Door of No Return.

I can hear the children on the other side calling to them, "Brothah, sistah, can I have . . . ?" The door shuts on their words. I cannot walk away, as if a chain has tethered me to another body. No one is there, yet they are all present.

My husband is the last to stay. He tries to place his hand on my shoulder, "Everyone has left babe." He gently tries to move me out. I aggressively ask him to go away. Though wrapped in love, his maleness interrupts a heaviness that I want to be weighted with. He clashes with the silent moans I let suffer through me. I want to be clothed in the anger, and washed over by my tears.

The day leading up to our visit to the Cape Coast Dungeon is a journey that leads us through the final steps enslaved Africans took before being shipped away from their land. Starting in Accra we take a two-hour bus ride into Assin Manso. Once there, the guide asks us all to remove our shoes, and we walk the highly vegetated trail barefoot. Some people refuse, stating poor health as a reason. I grow frustrated with excuses. There were none then when the old, sick, and abused were made to walk the asperous trail to their final bath. Who are we to say "no"?

We are such well-kept Americans— too comfortable, too removed. I have insect repellant soaking into my skin and more in my fanny pack. I should have let the mosquitos bite at my ankles and tear at my arms. Even the slightest external irritation would be appropriate, I think to myself. I want to run from them all, make it there first, and be alone with my feet planted under the water's mud.

But I am tied to the elder who steps slowly and takes rests on her walker. I am tied to the woman who has to take a picture with each step, slowing the journey. I am tied to my own unshakeable feelings of anxiety and annoyance.

This is a small likeness of the many people who were tied together and forced to walk in sync, no matter how discordant their gaits.

We reach the muddy waters and are told a piece of a chain was found below the surface just a few years ago. This is a grave site, unexcavated due to poor funding, unmarked due to the desire to move on from what hurts. The guide points to a clay hut we pass. Those who live there are known descendants of a person who was forcibly marched through this trail. He whispers this quietly. Repeating such things is insulting to them. They choose not to wear this fact with pride but shame.

Above the water's edge on a slight hill, an auction space for VIP slave owners still remains; there slavers got to pick the best Africans from among the general population. I find a seat on a rock between the silent river and the rampant one. I am in the intersection where some chose to risk their lives through escape. Many drowned who attempted to cross where I sat. I look left and stick my toe into the moving water on my right. Undecided on if, as a captive, I would have drowned or washed my body, I close my eyes, trying to decide. I collect water in an old baby oil bottle. Make a wish the guide says; anything comes true in these waters.

We arrive at the Cape Coast Dungeons and separate from the only white traveler. She is Jewish, and she believes she should be included. I want to humble her, but there is no need. It has already been arranged for her to take the tour separately. Thankfully, we are met by Sister Imakus, an expat and a healer, lovingly known as Mama Africa to the locals. She has been leading ceremonies for decades, and is there to help us process the tension. Lots of tight air passes through the dungeons, and we feed the space with offerings of rice and rum. We light candles under the clay heads lining the male dungeons. The glow brings the contorted faces to life. In the dim glow, they awake a deep anger inside me. I grow silent.

We have saved the flowered wreath for the women. Before entering their dungeon, we stop at a small entrance. There we learn the legend of Ashtua, who at 65 years old led frightened men in to battle against the British. The colonizers wanted the Ashanti's Golden Throne. Ashuta boldly resisted, giving up something so precious to her tribe. She was captured, but the throne remained with her people. The smallest room, a closet of space, was named after her by the whites. They would send rebellious African women there to punish them. Alone and dehydrated, they would more than likely die there—but what a victory death must feel like when the last drop of life is in the hands of slave owners.

This is when I am stung. A sharp pain circles my back, and I wonder if I did not eat enough. We walk to the female slave dungeons, and there I sit, never walking out of the Door of No Return. I still remain there in thought today. Not stuck, but willingly reliving all things I said to the spirits of the women. Though a year has passed, we are still in constant conversation. When I talk to myself, I now have thousands of ancestors who answer.

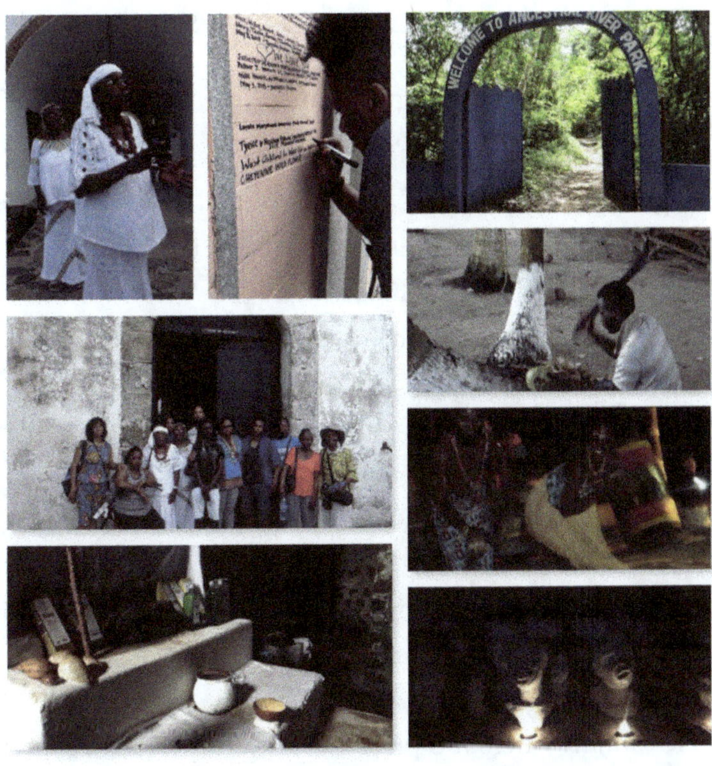

Left to Right

1. Sister Imakus not only hosted the poets at One Africa, she led the group in pouring libations for the ancestors at the Cape Coast Dungeons.
2. Wild- Flower signs the Assin Manso diaspora wall. The poets traveled to the site baptized as the "last bath." Here the ancestors took their final bath before being forced to walk miles to the slave dungeons. The water is known for healing, remembrance, and reclamation.
3. The blue arch marks the wooded trail that leads to the river where the final bath was taken by captured Africans. Poets walked the trail, barefoot, until their feet reached the water.
4. Standing outside of The Door of Return/No Return, Cape Coast Dungeons: Karla, Mama Makeda Sandra Hooper Mayfield, Sister Imakus, Nathan, Adeshima, Obi, Xiomara, Wild -Flower, Zakiyyah, and Wanda

Peach Orange Skies

Tyrice Deane Brown

Strange orange skies
    kids swinging low on branches of tall oak trees
        plummeting into cool blue waters
            as they surrender their bodies to torches
                of hot summer heat

Belly flops into open graves as the city burns from record highs
    flesh melts under flames of confederacy

It is a beautiful disaster of history
where my granny picked honeysuckles
    and her granny picked cotton
where running barefoot is preferred
    over the shackles of shoe laces
        matriarchs yell close the storm door!
            as dirty feet exit the place of no return

Sunday dinner cooks on the stove
    the aroma calling the outside dog
        to pace around the back porch
    ears perking as prayers to keep her safe and clean end with
        amens and off your elbows
yellow bones blacken quick under the pressure of
    colorism at the dinner table

I come from young stretched skin—tiny frames
    carrying marked bellies,
        targets for new oppression
sisters gather supporting her squat, as she, like sumo,
    wrestles pain and burden into the world

I come from long runs in the woods
    with galloping dogs at ashed heels
Breaking record times as the wind tries
    to catch hold of quick legs like whips on bare hides
        "I see your hiney. It's nice and shiny.
            If you don't hide it, I'm gonna bite it!"

Echoes through hiding places as play breaks the reality of dusk
    freedom crawls in the tall grass
        long talks with caterpillars and fireflies
Past the time of segregation
    ladybugs and deer sit on the doorstep
    as honey sweet dew captures
        the James River in tiny bubbles

I come from sitting in between her soft brown thighs
    as she greases my scalp and hums
        cigarette smoke mixing with my hair as she inhales
            with every note of the song and twist of her hand

I come from down home
    deep down home

so deep lights don't twinkle brighter than the stars

I come from sin and pleasure
    grinding to slow jams in basement parties
        his hot breath on your neck
            switches when you come home nine months late

I come from   **the SOUTH.**

From the Loins of Yaa Asantewaa

Jewell King-Speaks

I come from the South.
I come from the East.
I come from the North.
I come from the West.

Seen as the worst being, they said nothing good can come out
of me.
But one evening Eve grew from my ribcage,
Brought forth forbidden fruits.
She took a bite and invited me to a feast,
Which got us kicked out of Eden to Earth.

We are the first astronauts to discover Earth without a rocket
but on foot.
I am crazily amazing.
I come from excellence.
Stronger than Neil Armstrong,
I am the first black guy to walk on the moon with black shoes
and white socks, but I backslide when I do the moon walk,
Bleached the truth and ended my life,
Forgetting that we are black, coz life isn't fair.

I come from today.

I come from tomorrow.
Both tomorrow and today have got a two, to, too.
So, if tomorrow never comes then today never comes, too.
We've been living a dream that never came to pass,
But my yesterday hunted my today with an arrow, so I
screamed for tomorrow.
That was a trap because tomorrow never comes.
I come from nowhere.

I come from the loins of Yaa Asantewaa,
The brave woman that led an army to war,
I come from Yaa Asantewaa.
I come from Sarah Baartman,
The actual Baartman before the fictional Batman,
The woman who was degraded and disgraced by the Western-
ers,
Simply because she had big lips, big breasts, big buttocks, and
wide hips.
I think she was the first woman stripped naked and placed on
display against her will.
But today our black women do it willingly thinking their but-
tocks are their greatest asset,
But instead they are disgracing my origin.

I come from Sarah Baartman,
I come from Black.
I am the night in the beginning that paved way for the light.
I wasn't greedy.

I am the moon.
I am darkness.
I come from a place that makes everyone stagger in jealousy.

I come from Africa,

Where civilization began without guns,
Where Madagascar, the island, saw into the future and prophe-
sied way before prophets.
This is where we drink from supernatural cups.
We drink from the horn of Africa.

I come from Africa.

Letter to

Tyrice Deane Brown

You found it there
Cropped like belly tops on hot city days

It looked lopsided
One strand unfitted around uneven curves

It seemed loose, forgotten like one sock stuck in the dryer the
match long gone
So you thought it would be ok to take it
Rework some fabric so it fit you only

It became your go-to item
Like a little black dress
Every girl has to have

But when the buttons popped leaving your skin exposed
There lay an un-seaming sight

Each thread had been a vein
A blood-pulsing, life-giving vein
And you had cut through the main artery

You had been rocking skin as your silk
Hair as your fur
Lashes as your feathers

You tied fingers around your waist
Stuffed yourself into bones like a corset

Your best outfit is another's shell
Fossilized into a decaying fortress

You are immortalized by living dead.

Letter to the Police

Jewell King-Speaks

I walked past my past to present my tensed present,
The one that was molested and brought to its knees by the
man in uniform
       so inasmuch as I was reduced in height
       I was looked down upon like I'm the syndrome,

So, when I came face to face with the gun
       I asked him to shoot the video of my life
       to set me free from this prison cage of a body,

And he reduced my height in life coz he shot that gun,
And this new life begun.

Coz I was set free and remember I won't be killed again
       coz spirits don't die,
       so I lived on.

I'm convinced these men are just criminals in uniforms
       empowered by the government,
       and this is what I meant.

Coz if nature could cardiac arrest me
for stealing a man's elbows as armed robbery,
Then nature is a better police than
Men who stand by the roadside to get one *cedi* from me.

10

Poetry Slam Prepping

Zakiyyah G. E. Capehart

The main event of the West Oakland to West Africa Poetry Exchange Group's journey to Ghana arrived at last. It was the day we had been planning for a year. Not only do we get to perform our poetry for the Ghanaian audience, but we get to perform with our poet partner. I wondered how we would be received by an unfamiliar audience, on a different continent. Will they like our poetry? The thought made me nervous.

It occurred to me that the other poets were probably having similar thoughts, but my roommate Makeda seemed relaxed and confident. Although our room was on the second floor, the same floor as Wild-Flower, Imani, and Xiomara, I hadn't seen them during the first part of the day. So, I didn't have a sense of how they were feeling. Nor had I spoken with Karla, Wanda, Tyrice, or Marcus aka Adeshima—the poets on the first floor. Before long, Karla came upstairs looking a little stressed. When I saw her later, she said, some of the poets were having difficulty selecting their poems.

What poems should I recite? Should I wear a dress or pants? The locks of my hair were styled up uniquely, crowning my head. I considered taking them down. But I changed my mind; it would be too much trouble.

I needed a secluded area to select and practice my poems. Then I recalled the perfect spot. At the Agoo Hostel where we were staying in Accra, there was an outdoor porch area in the back. I had gone there a couple of times, to be alone. No one was ever there. I used that space to prepare myself.

The Poetry Slam was scheduled to begin at six twenty-nine in the evening. Our event would take place at the W.E.B Du-Bois Memorial Centre, a short distance from where we were staying. W.E.B DuBois' Memorial Centre is a historical, educational, and spiritually inspiring centre. Our group visited and had a fabulous time. It would be great being there again. Since our event would take place in the evening, we had most of the day to prepare ourselves. The WO2WA Slam Championship Poetry Exchange Project with Ehalakasa awaited!

See a Way Through

Nora Anyidoho, aka Xorlarlie

When we look in each other's eyes,
Will we see a way through?
When you look into my eyes, what will you see?
Will you see answers to my questions?
Will you see the thing around my neck? How tight is it?

Will you see strength and resilience in eyes that don't cry?
Or will you see broken tear glands?

Will you see bravery or fear?

Will you see my dark companions?
Will you see my demons, like fever—gone by morning?

When you look into my eyes,
Will you know that I am dying?
That I am living? That I am weak? That I am strong?

Do you think I need God? Do you think I will do just fine?

Can you answer my questions?

Do you know me now?

Advice on Vivisection

Sara Biel

Do you know me now?
Now that my skin is peeled back?
Layers of muscle folded aside.

What can be discovered
With this maze of calamity laid bare?
It is pockmarked—mysterious as a harvest moon.

"Don't waste the exquisite crest," she says.
"Don't shy from the rush of pain before the crash."
Hear your gasp of terror
Your roar of venomous rage.
Name the memories that leave you
Sunblind
Sputtering in confusion.
Caress your clench of grief before the release
A wail full enough for drowning.

Here,
Inside,
In your innermost inky fist
Is a virgin breath of resuscitation.
The genesis of selfish compassion.

These tenacious words grip my sweat slick heart
Drag me clear of my own history.
Now I can be the exception to my own most Disastrous Rules.

Love's Rules

Nora Anyidoho, aka Xorlarlie

Now I can be the exception to my own most Disastrous Rules.

Rule No. 1: FLEE FROM THE TRIGGERS.
And what have I to say but:
HERE I AM
With You; my most volatile trigger.

Rule No. 2: DON'T YOU CRY; EVEN WHEN IT HURTS
And, how well have I adhered to this!
Remained tight-lipped while you slipped my heart out of my
chest,
Wrapped it safely in red silk
Secured it in a velvety box by your bedside
To idolize it every night
Remained dry-eyed,
As I crawled through life
"heartless." Depthless.
Giving you my heart hurt,
But I dared not cry,
Till tonight.

Rule No. 3: LOVE WHOLE-HEARTEDLY.
And I do, don't I?

I let you keep my heart. All of it.
Forgetting that I will need a piece of it,
To breathe. To live.
Giving you my heart is enough, right?
Giving you my already broken heart should be enough.
And you do love me too, don't you?
Love me so hard. So much to
Stash my heart in a velvety casket by your bedside.
To adore every night. Only.
But I dared not ask for a piece of it back.
Until tonight.
Tonight I ask for all of it.

Rule No. 4: DON'T GIVE YOUR HEART TO THE BRO-
KEN.
This rule I broke from the very start
When I first gave you my heart.

For who else can know what it feels like to be broken than the
broken?
Who else can learn how to love the broken but the broken?
And who else can mend the broken but the broken?
And how right I was!

And how wrong I am!
My heart is safe, inside its casket, beside your bed.
Safe.
Dispensable.
Contingently loved, but still loved. Somehow.
And how can I blame you?
What can one do with a heart this broken?
Kintsukuroi, maybe?

But where is your gold?

EDITOR'S NOTE: In Japan, *kintsukuroi* is the art of mending pottery with lacquer resin that has been infused with silver or gold. This art form is often associated with philosophical metaphors.

Where Is Your Gold?

Sara Biel

Where is your gold?
It is not in your heart.
There is no gold there but a yawning cave,
a place waiting to be filled, brimming with shadows.
Shadows that swim through nothingness knocking want from
side to side.

Is it in your hands?
Sticky little fingers crush it to your vacuous center.
Squinting eyes on guard for who might take what you've been
handed.
"Sad." It doesn't hold your small sweaty hand does it?
You grab it tightly.
Your gold knows no loyalty; even now it is squirming from
your grip.

Is your gold under your feet?
A road to guide your movements, to show you the way.
An uncanny journey that cannot be softened.
Not in this cacophony you cultivate to hide confusion.
Would you follow the path and take it up or
lock it up so it just is—meaning and purpose nullified.

Is your gold just a mask?
A pretense of value. A con called purity. A hiding place.
You could be anyone or no one.
You live hidden within a falling tower.
A false front hoping to dazzle, always to dazzle,
so that nobody will know your hollow eyes are just hollow.

Is your gold just a shell? It is already chipping. Flaking away,
revealing an ordinary old man,
tired and lost without the distraction of twittering crowds,
the blown blindness of the lights.

When this time is past, when its color is gone,
when your gold's tarnished by too many grabbing hands—
what will you be?

Crumpled yellow foil littering the corner of an empty room.
Or even an embarrassing memory of a wasted time.

Left to Right

1. You will need a friend who knows how to navigate the intricate complexities of the Makala Market. Chris, an expert artist and shop owner, not only helped Karla through the market, he guided the entire group each day of the trip.
2. While in Cape Coast the poets were hosted at One Africa. Each dwelling is named with purpose, here Karla stands outside of her lodging.
3. Adeshima, Akambo and Deydzi are pictured strategizing over their poetic delivery.
4. Zakkiyah gathering with Ghanaian youth on the sands of the Atlantic.

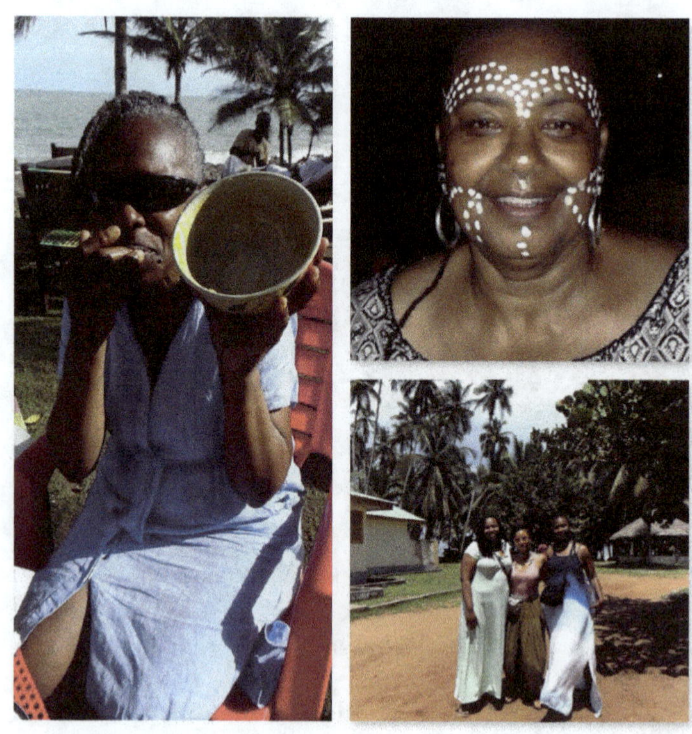

Left to Right

1.   Like Zakiyyah, all the poets enjoyed tasting the joys of Sankofa.
2.   Mama Makeda adorned in tribal face paint.
3.   On the shores of home: Xiomara, Tyrice, and Imani

Competition—All in Fun

Karla Brundage

We arrived, and we were nervous. The 2018 Ghana/ US Poetry Slam Event was about to commence. What did it mean that some people from the United States, specifically Oakland, would be throwing down some lyrics in the oral tradition, challenging this Ghanaian crew?

We gathered at the W. E. B. Du Bois Center, on an outdoor stage under a large tree. The outdoor venue provided an atmosphere of the village. We also had stage lights, a microphone, and chairs.

Sir Black arranged for some of the students of Ghanatta Performing Arts High School to present an original play of theirs promoting equal education for differently abled students. The students enthusiastically performed traditional dances with drumming.

As the sun began to set, the audience arrived. The onlookers included a variety of people from supporters and fans of Ehalakasa, to a group from the U.S. Embassy, a few taxi drivers, and curious onlookers.

Two emcees explained the rules of a poetry slam. Each poem can be no longer than three minutes. There will be five judges from the audience that score each poem on a scale of 1-10. The highest and lowest scores are ignored; then a composite score is added up. In some competitions, there are teams; in others, it is by the individual. Sir Black and I have agreed this will be a team challenge, similar to a cross-country meet, where all the points are added up. Each contribution will count.

The lights went on! My stomach churned with anticipation. After a week of touring and fun, sharing words and stories, we were at the poetry competition. Who would win—Ghana or the U.S.? The Ehalakasa team, or the WO2WA team?

She Paved the Way:
Dominique Folloroux-Ouattara

Azi Edoua

She paved the way through
since he became President and
she became First Lady of Cote d'Ivoire.

You only hear about her when it concerns child welfare
her charity foundation's name: Children of Africa.

She paved the way through
and is still doing it right now
helping children through an ophthalmic caravan.

In 6 years,
it's the fifth medical mission.
After 15 years in blindness, for some children
it's their first time to see.

Blindness

Noemi Rose Gonzalez-Barillas

it's their first time to see
eyes colored in blind
shutters closed
hearts raining
thundering tear storm

two locked arms
carry a key to freedom
if embrace
left that invisible ventricle
back in childhood

chambers never searched for
a custom to which they
weren't accustomed
dating dropped
mating lost

children never came
baby rocking
some tree topping
for formula
no taste

reflection missed
eyes never kissed
baby in rushes
old tale's true
lullaby reeds

singing currents to shores
milky welcome
cranes wander round
whisper futures *gone mute*

When I Saw You

Azi Edoua

Gone mute
My mind
My endless thoughts running, playing, dancing
Schemes, malicious ideas, interesting stories

Gone mute
When I saw you, beautiful, free spirit, giggling and laughing
Spinning around and around and around

Gone mute
You and your carefreeness
I gave you my heart to love, my freedom in slavery
I received nothing—call me unloved

Gone mute
My treasured feelings
Just gone

Lost Love

Noemi Rose Gonzalez-Barillas

just gone
one day you see your beloved
until you don't

just gone
like a father out to other pastures
yours already shorn

just gone
can't see forgiveness
for all the just-gone-wrongs

around meals that were not made
through schools where children saved
stories about fathers who stayed
and pride and lions strutting blind

to seeing children the ones of your own seed
not even a register
of wishes gone unheeded

Father, Papi, my mother's first turned worst

why was the sacrifice your children
we can't see your love
maybe you never had it

is that what we must divine
or is it your wish
for your children to be blind

love opens in our hearts
like hollering sunshine
we seek shade as solace

The Poetry Slam

Zakiyyah G. E. Capehart

Our long-awaited moment had come into fruition. The West Oakland to West Africa Poetry Exchange Group and the Ehalakasa poetry group, began by reciting poetry with their poet partner. This demonstrated the *renshi*-style of poetry that the two groups wrote in, and exchanged poetry with, for approximately one year.

Then the Slam began. For this part of the program there is audience participation. The poets must abide by the rules of the Slam to receive their points from the audience's vote. The Group with the highest score is the winner. And the winning team receives a prize. The entire process is quick paced, fun, competitive, and exhilarating.

In the end, the Ehalakasa Group won the Poetry Slam; however, they only won by one point!

This was the West Oakland to West Africa Poetry Exchange Group's first international performance together on the African continent. In addition, the first collective Poetry Slam with the Ehalakasa poet partners. Henceforth the groups will be on the map.

There is no stopping us now!

His Other Lover

Karla Brundage

My lover has a lover.
She fits so nicely into the palm of his hand
like my breasts.
He loves to talk to her quietly and often
goes into another room to be on her.
They sometimes quarrel when he turns
her off, and then the house is
quiet except for an occasional mumble
as she fights to arouse him.

How can I live with her in the house?
But it is not only the house because
he carries her with him all the time
in his jacket pocket,
and they keep secrets from me,
clandestine messages only they share.

At dinner, he ignores her,
but I sense her presence.
I long to have a chance alone with her,
Like him, it is nearly impossible.
She is lovely, her voice unobtrusive, and
she often sings a little song.
She can change her colors

and often wears bright flashy accessories.

Unlike me, he can shut her off at will.
I am not so easy to control.
He says he loves me,
yet when he holds me
I can feel him thinking of her
and what messages she may hold
what secret better passions she may possess.

Passion

Sir Black, aka Yibor Kojo Yibor

What secret better passions she may possess?

That was my question to her
the night she left to buy the latest iPhone.

You see I am not that blind,
even though I use dark glasses by night.

Truth is she is the YOLO generation,
chasing the mirage of reality
connecting with what was, what could be
and intangibilities.

So I ask myself, are we better off in the abstract?
Have humans really improved
since the introduction of laptops?

The world has shrunken into a small unit
interconnected via easy mobility and electronic transport.
Loneliness has been healed
by virtual and mechanical escorts in the form of dildos,
artificial vags, and digital porn shops.

Emotions are now being expressed and sought in smileys

and short codes like *lol, lmao, smh, gm,* and *wtf.*

With mobile text messages powerful enough
To caress a lover's G-spot—what a shame!

If technology has increased interconnectivity,
why is my mobility limited
to stamps on display in my passport?

If modernization is inevitable
then so is technology and everything that comes with it.

But posterity is right to question "tech-with-no-logic"
since courting right and wrong
still remains an expensive luxury.

Although I always stand to be corrected, I will still insist:
it is only when you and I talk, hold, kiss, caress,
and make consensual love
that I feel truly connected.

The Present

Karla Brundage

I am
the present
the gift of the here and now—
the love we give in the moment
under the shining sun is the gift.

When under the mango tree
gentle rain falls, cleansing
the dust off tattered leaves,
stand tall,

hold your shoulders back,
imagine a light from your head to the sky,
open your throat chakra, and
listen with your voice.

Surround yourself with a shawl
of moonbeams, let butterflies
into your soul, and be thankful
in rainbow colors.

Your ancestors gave you life,
and soon you will be one, too.
Give back to the community
with deeds not words.

May your prayers be grateful.
You have so many talents.
Open your soul to the
ocean of love before you.

Before You

Sir Black, aka Yibor Kojo Yibor

before you
was time and chance
space and movement
and other elements
tangible and intangible

some for delight and some for disgust
some lived long some longed to live
some came and claimed in the name of pain
some survived and stayed alive
some wept and some slept

however none before you
was allowed to allow chance to time
either to appear or disappear
in space or in movement
except with the elements of sleep

now at the end of the beginning
for all those who made it here or there
and those who could not or did not exist
let it be made known
to you all and them all

that it was not about who or what
to have passed through here or there
rather time and chance happened
day and night comes
life and death passed

1. The Ghanaian community volunteered to vote for their favorite poets during the WO2WA- Ehalakasa Poetry Slam.
2. Students from the community blessed the slam event with music and dance.
3. Ehalakasa took home the winning palm seed, but everybody wins when the diaspora connects! Seen here; Deydzi, Xiomara, Nora, Jewell- King Speaks, Sabukei, 100%, Tyrice, Natty, Wild-Flower, Obi, Adesihma, Zakiyyah, Mama Makeda, Karla, Wanda, Imani, Faiba, Philipa, Front row (kneeling): Joseph, Karl, Akambo.

Poets from both countries are forever grateful to Karla and Sir Black. As poets themselves, they shared their work during the slam. As leaders, they empowered the group to stretch beyond their comfort zones. It is clear that their vision and dedication to the culture and craft is one born from love and kinship.

Top Left to Bottom Right

Just a few of the poets from Ehalakasa that blessed the stage with rage, passion, love, and exceptional craft and style.

1. Nora, 2. Faiba, 3. 100%, 4. Sabukie, 5. Philipa

After Ghana Reflections

Makeda, aka Sandra Hooper Mayfield

I was born in America in 1951, but my life truly began with our trip to Ghana. I had just gotten the news that I had fourth-stage renal cancer. I could not believe that I was going to die without realizing my dream of traveling to Africa.

I was planning my memorial when I received a call from an old friend, inviting me to participate in a poetry exchange between Ehalakasa, a deep and soulful group of poets whom I LOVE from Ghana and WO2WA, a gathering of eclectic people from the East Bay, who have become family.

In that first meeting, we briefly discussed the possibility of travelling to Ghana. It was in that moment my life began for real. I did not know the journey home would not be about death but about healing. What appeared to be a death sentence became freedom and a new life.

When I set foot on African soil, I began to rest from all that had happened to my people since they were first stolen. One day, I was sitting on a shore near the Atlantic Ocean. It was hot and humid, and a gentle breeze went through me. I felt a healing in my mind, body, and spirit, and I knew I was home. I knew the Truth. I was born in America but I belong to Africa. And all this time I had been walking to Ghana.

The doctors say I am in remission. I say I am healed, and I am in the process of making Africa home again. My soul is appreciative to Karla, our fearless leader. I am forever grateful for her courage.

I thank The Power that Lives within us.

Day-Dreaming

Makeda, aka Sandra Hooper Mayfield

When I get to Ghana

Ima wrap myself in six yards of white cotton
Wear beads, anklets, bracelets, and sometimes Ima wear a crown,

Ima garden barefoot, under the influence of moonlit music
and ju ju.

When I get to Ghana

Ima cook gumbo and jollof, an my house go smell like,
"You wanna stay forever."

Ima sit wide-legged on the shore, exhale hate and breathe Africa.

Then Ima lay down and let the ebb and flow wash the white away.

When I get to Ghana

Ima fall in black black black Love, let him press his body on mine,

Then Ima sit on his lap, swing my feet,

And feed us some watermelon.

Ghana, Oh Ghana!

Zakiyyah G. E. Capehart

traveling by air
across the sea
journey of a lifetime
finally coming to be
land of my ancestors
history awaits
unveiling roots
opening wounds
where scars
are left to heal
weaving spirits
and touching souls
Ghana Oh Ghana
constantly on my mind
when i arrive
what do i hope to find
will you be there
waiting to welcome
and receive me
with embracing arms
will i feel your love
running through me
until my cup
runneth over

here i sit
staring out at clouds
silently praying
Ghana Oh Ghana
your distant disconnected
family is now returning home
to a country once thought of
as the
Land of no return.

The Door of Return

Marcus Lorenzo Penn, aka Adeshima

Up up and away in a plane to dear Ghana
I am returning home again.

Representing a land of oaks
I come to join my West African country folks.

11 years ago I came as a stranger
And now I come back as a family member.

Brothers and sisters, mothers and misters
We are all now so familiar.

I bring a gift of words that have not been heard
Like sounds of a distant bird.

West Oakland to West Africa is the journey I've travelled
With our group cultural connections have unraveled.

Bonds have formed, and friendships have grown

In brotherhood/sisterhood, we now call our own.

We're not in competition, but to share our composition
Through word, thought, opinion, and vision.

This exchange brings change to hearts, minds, and souls.
No matter young, old, shy, bold, we've a story to be told.

We're here, and this is us
No matter if we've come here by plane, train, or bus.

Family is family, love and acceptance.
Despite mistakes, we've repentance, not a jail sentence.

We come from lives of loss and gain, joys and pain
Learning again and again.

Our ancestors guide and reach us in our hearts
Even through life's roughest parts.

Experiences add color to our living
Much like an artist adds color to a painting.

We're all artists painting a perfect picture,
Weaving a delicate tapestry, creating a mosaic.

But our art doesn't require us to display.
All it asks is for us to stay.

I'm Home

Wild-Flower Brashear

Day-o
Day-o
Daylight come and
We wan' go home

I'm home

Sorry, I could not make it home any sooner
But this is the first time
I could make it, back and
Pull away from the binds and ties
That have prevented me
From this journey, so

Sorry, I'm late

But this has been the only time
That I could make it back
In 400 years

To transform centuries of compounded miseries
Composed of collected tears

This paralyzing fear
Of never returning here

But the true definition
Of our ancestors' resilience
Is reaching Africa's shores
Through their descendants

A generational longing to reconnect

This is our ancestral privilege

The ability to
Carry both pain and hope
In the same breath

And in that same breath
Being raped and beaten
Until we had no breath
And when there was no breath
There was remembrance of essence breathing
New life into the next generation's first breath
And in the first breath
We carry the world's burden until there is no breath
Struggling to reach these shores before our last breath, so

I'm sorry, I'm late

I think of you
When the sun sets

Day-o
Day-o
Daylight come and

I'm home

In exactly 400 years
Next year
Since the first
African reached
The shores of Jamestown, Virginia in 1619

We shed our skin in that earth
Watered their crops with our blood
Broke our bones and bodies
To erect institutions to lives on our backs

And we are still here

We've been
Implanting the spiritual seeds
Of one day returning
To a sky
And land
Familiar

We've been beaten bloody
Until consciousness is lost
Then found
In Sankofa's
Ingrained spiritual
Synchronicities
Of our mind's third—eye planes
Giving us the ambition
To do more than just maintain, so

I'm sorry I'm late

They'd have us believe
We've been away
Too long
As if my spirit stopped fighting to return
Home

They'd have me believe
That y'all sold me off
Severing my ties to
My birthright

When All of Africa is my home

They'd have me believe
That when I came back
Being a descendant
Of my ancestors' dreams

That fought for me to be free
And return me back to a
Point they knew
They'd never return

That you would never
Receive me
Acknowledge me
Hold onto me
Hug me
And kiss me
Recognizing
Our shared history

But that I am a stranger
Disconnected

An unrecognizable entity

So
I'm sorry
I'm late

I had
To take
My time
To recollect

While I collect
The remnants
Of my grandmothers' and grandfathers'
Fragmented spirits

Accra,

CENTER OF THE EARTH!!!

I bring forth our ancestors who fought for me to be free,
and return them back to the point they'd thought they never
reach.

They shackled me
Stole me
Branded me
Shipped me
Worked me
Bred me
Lynched me
And never returned me

So I'm sorry

I couldn't make it home any sooner

So sorry I am late
First, I had to return myself to myself

Unapologetic

Makeda, aka Sandra Hooper Mayfield

I am not sorry, I gave it up
like liquor
nicotine
making bad boys king
and nights that stole the years

I am not sorry, I'm good
like early morning lovin
nappy hair
girls with daddy's
Nana's peach cobbler
things that dried my tears

I am not sorry, I'm living in the plus
spittin poetry
lovin hard
dissin the c-word
sitting on the porch in my slip
copacetic things that ice my fears

I'm not sorry, I'm authentic
like slow dancing
sporting locks
laughing loud

Oozing Black
saying fin to
doing JuJu
and other things that make jungle dust
if want to

I'm not sorry
I am courage
like
mama dead
daddy gone
12 feeling on my own
16 pregnant
Bury the middle sister
survive the divorce
bury the daddy
survive survive survive
bury the big sister

Living every day anyway
and other strengths that slayed the fear

I am not sorry
I'm light
in the dark
blinding, shining
turn me on light

Like the sun every every every day
shining light for me to see
what my life could truly be
and other notes that dance on fear

I am not sorry
I am Divine
like an eclipse,
or a hood miracle
harvested organs
that take my breath
and give it back again

I am not sorry
I am Love
pour me out
scrape the bowl
lick the spoon love

Ain't too proud to beg love
ride or die love
down in the country with the elders' love
forgiving incest
raggedy drawers but the kids go to private school love
8 rock love
forgiving rape love

Didn't eat last night, but the baby did love

surviving slavery love

Taking your whooping
everlasting love

Pushing out a baby love
blacker the berry love
hanging from a tree love

Take a knee
die at the Lorraine Hotel love
forgive myself love
hang on a cross and die love
and other truths that saved my life

I'm not sorry
I'm free   Unapologetically

1. Back in Oakland poets Adeshima, Zakkiyah, Wanda, Xiomara, Radhiyah, Sara and Karla reunite after the Sankofa.
2. Though not all poets could make the trip to Ghana, poets Radhiyah (Picture 2) and Tamaris (Picture 3) were two of the voices that were carried in spirit.
3. Zakiyyah, Donte Clark, Mimi, Marcus Lorenzo Penn aka Adeshima, Mama Makeda Sandra Hooper Mayfield and Karla, joined together to view Donte's newest film. Donte is a Bay Area activist who creates art that supports unity and growth in the Black community.

EHALAKASA
WEST
OAKLAND
VRS WEST
AFRICA
SLAM
CHAMPIONSHIP
POETRY EXCHANGE PROJECT
SUN. MAY
20TH 2018
6:29PM
Du Bois
Center
CANTONMENTS
For more info: 020 5043890

Afterword

By Kathryn Waddell Takara, PhD

The significance of this successful project and book, *Our Spirits Carry Our Voices*, affirms Black people as trailblazers, as movers and shakers who serve local, national, and international communities to educate the public in cultural traditions, and explore the relativity of the black cosmos, including creativity, conservation and inspiration.

The creator of the West Oakland to West Africa project (WO2WA), Karla Brundage, had a vision to establish collaborative partnerships and international, cultural communication in the United States and West Africa, through poetry.

The humanistic aim was to enhance the growing sense of interconnectedness between West African and West Oakland poets and intellectuals, artists and leaders. To this end, the participants were mainly from the Bay Area in Northwest California, Ghana and the Ivory Coast. The planning, outreach, implementation, methodology, and humanistic approach attracted 25 participants who shared Karla's cross-cultural vision of connecting through writing and technology.

The excited, expectant participants in the project rallied to the call, using their eyes, ears, historical and cultural myths and legends to create a collection of collaborative poetry by sharing new paradigms of history and self-worth, and uncover the unforeseen value of the experience: the dual nature of identity, disparate connections, and the value of interconnectedness. They engaged these themes by using Renshi poetry as an accessible, concrete medium to create new skills, and evoke an expanded identity using threads of associative thought.

One of the results poets experienced, after a year of working on this creative project, was a momentous spiritual journey back home where some uncovered their ancestral roots. Not surprisingly, these poets were able to experience the restoration of identity and empowerment through their exploration of selfhood, ancestry, history and culture. And, all the poets endeavored to untangle symbolic language and understand behavior patterns that transcend linear time.

In all of their looking backwards and forward, these poets used modern vehicles of education, technology, email, Skype and travel. The reimagining of a future filled with arts using technology, a resource for history and tradition, as seen through a black lens was part of Karla's visionary project.

This collection falls into the category of the newly coined phrase, Afrofuturism.

Afrofuturism is a fusion of new and old forms, taking observations of traditional art forms to create new riffs, often political, while conserving some of the more traditional means and themes of expression. It is a cultural aesthetic and even a philosophy of history that develops and cultivates intersections of vanguard visionary and experimental modes with traditional art forms using technology to enhance interconnectedness.

Blacks remain central, in the vanguard: visionary, experimental, ahead of time, yet deeply rooted in tradition (legacy) and improvisation. Afrofuturism is inventive and original. It is spiritual, relying on imaginative interpretations of reality using reflections on dreams, myths, and history. There is an Afrocentric cosmology that in various ways describes the universe and our human place in it.

Afrofuturism invites participation, evoking interactive engagement with the other. It is creatively centered in all areas of human activity with a shared aim of envisioning black futures that stem from an Afro-Diasporic tradition and shared experiences, somewhat intuitive, whether consciously or not.

It inevitably includes Afro-isms: oral expression, creativity, legends, myths, proverbs, metaphors, symbols, and art in new forms. It is a creative psychological storytelling through carving words, songs and dance, into recognizable and unrecognizable manifestations. It is a labyrinth of questioning and exchange. It calls into question: What is reality and how does it differ across cultures?

Afrofuturism also uses humor and a sense of balance to create a dynamic, psychological force field, spiritual and healing - nurturing the heart and soul of community (local, national, international) and identity, the inner country with a vibrant, sometimes loving energy. The form becomes restorative, inviting harmonic innovations, angular rhythms, and hope for a more compassionate, understanding world.

Our Spirits Carry Our Voices is significant on many levels. It is a verification of the possibility of connections in a turbulent world. The presence of mostly African American and African voices reflecting on common themes such as the African Diaspora, identity, family, and the visible and invisible worlds, shows the power of partnering, interconnectedness, and enhanced understanding between cultures, histories and reflections. The responsible reader will recognize the rich resources of the huge and ancient continent of Africa, and how Africans were essential and indispensable to the building and prosperity of capitalism, the USA and Europe.

Finally, the strong leadership and creative genius of the creator and organizer of this project was superb. Karla Brundage, a biracial woman who identifies as African American, was born to diversity. Through growing up in Hawai`i, being educated on the East Coast, settling and working in California, and living in Africa for four years, she has become a political and spiritual citizen of the world who has the courage invite others to observe and explore differences, internal and external, while exerting strong leadership. Her awareness of the power of exchange to support world peace, lends credence to the validation of communication, trading stories, and sharing life through poetry and friendships. Karla's poetic sensibilities made this project successful, resulting in the group travel to Ghana to meet their poetic partners and this book, *Our Spirits Carry our Voices.*

About the Contributors

Emmanuel Akambo, Jr. is a Ghanaian Slam poet. He started writing poetry in 2015 after winning the international Slam during the Global Issue Service Summit (GISS) Conference. He has performed in Cote d'Ivoire, Ghana, and Germany. He believes that, just like God, we owe it to ourselves to "create" before leaving Earth. "So I write, I speak."

Nora (Xorlarlie) Anyidoho is a young Ghanaian poet and spoken word artist. She is a member of the Ehalakasa poetry group, and has performed her poetry to diverse audiences. She also dabbles in other forms of art such as ink sketches and portrait drawings. When Xorlarlie is not sketching, writing or musing over words, she is grappling with numbers and is building a career as a financial analyst.

Dodzi Korsi Aveh, aka WhoIsDeydzi Dodzi Korsi Aveh, is a graduate of University of Ghana Graduate, in Theatre Arts and English Language with a focus on Creative Writing and Filmmaking. He has been writing and performing Spoken Word poetry for seven years. He has been active in the following art communities: Nsadwase Nkomo, Ehalakasa, and Sankofa Sessions. In 2018, he launched his first Spoken Word album titled SoundMind. It consists of 19 original Spoken Word pieces all centered on mental health issues in Ghana. In 2019 he released his first short film entitled "Green Green Grasses" that explores the misconceptions Africans on the continent of Africa have about life for black people in Europe and America vs. the realities. He teamed up with Philipa Gyamfi for the Ehalakasa Environ Womental Slam 2019 and won. He is currently working on his next studio Album titled 4 Sheygey reasons, which should be ready in 2020.

Radhiyah Ayobami was born in Brooklyn by way of the South. She is an Africana Studies graduate of Brooklyn College and a prose MFA graduate of Mills College in Oakland, CA. She has been published in several journals including Kweli, Agni, and Tayo Literary Magazine, and has facilitated writing workshops with pregnant teens, inmates and elders. She has received fellowships from the New York Foundation for the Arts, Sustainable Arts Foundation and Atlantic Center for the Arts. She is a Reiki Master, an herbal tea blender, a listener of the trees, and Mama to a beautiful son. Her first book is *the long amen.*

Sara Biel is a poet, visual artist, and social worker. Her work combines original text with many different art materials. She is passionate about collaborative art and performance processes, and she focuses on art as a medium for building community. Sara's work has been featured in Oakland's Moondrop Productions reading series and Sparkle and Blink. She is the editor of Colossus: Bay Are Poets Challenge Immigration Injustice. Sara and her artistic collaborator Karla Brundage curated and produced of the Temescal Insitu project in the fall of 2013.

Wild-Flower Brashear said, "My mother always told me that there was a lot of life in the desert. I, Wild-Flower, "Flower," as my daddy would call me with a thick country accent, took root in Death Valley's desert. Born to Phyllis, a woman with clear eyes and a clear soul, and Lafayette, a Black cowboy from Texas, I was raised an eighties baby in the heart and soul of Leimert Park, South Central Los Angeles. I was surrounded by a strong Black artist community connected to our African roots. Leimert Park fed and nurtured me. The elders gave me the creative nutrients to grow confident with tradition and vision. You could walk the streets and see jazz notes reverberating through the trees. I remember being woken up by the bold bass of the Djembe drum every Sunday. I shared my first poems on Billy Higgins' World Stage on Degnan Blvd. Spoken Word connects my pen to the stories of our ancestors. It offers the messages of our past in our present to guide and preserve our future.

Tyrice Deane Brown is an MFA graduate with a degree in Creative Writing and Poetry. She writes from an identity-focused lens, one that draws from her existence navigating in America as a Black woman. As a dedicated educator she now works as an English Adjunct Professor at Northern Virginia Community College, and she is working on her first book about the history of her hometown, Lynchburg, Virginia. She hopes to create spaces of learning and light that uplift the very topics she writes on ... {black}identity.

Zakiyyah G. E. Capehart is a poet/storyteller, performing artist, visual artist, and radio producer and host. She is from New York where she studied at Henry Street Settlement, Frank Silver's Workshop, and HB Studio. She has performed her poetry at the Brooklyn Moon Cafe, and other venues in the New York Tri-State area. In 2002 she relocated to the Bay Area with her husband Bryant. While living in Oakland she studied at the Stagebridge Theatre Company. As a member of the Writer's Workshop at the Downtown Oakland Senior Center, recites her poetry at their Book Launches and Poetry Salons. Her poetry is published in several anthologies. She is also a member of the Cousin Zica Writer's Group. Zakiyyah is a two-time grantee of funds from the Akonadi Foundation. Currently she is working on the publication of her first book of poems and short stories.

Azi Edoua lives in Abidjan, Cote d'Ivoire

Noemi Rose Gonzalez-Barillas is a poet, freelance journalist, comedian, activist, and event producer who has achieved a lifelong goal of earning an MFA in Creative Writing in 2018. Each of us needs to express ourselves creatively. It's an inherent drive Mimi respects, as every individual struggles to discover and free their voice. Writing has been her way both in and out. Since 2014, she has participated in and conducted writing workshops.

Xiomara is a poet and fiction writer from Los Angeles and holds a BA in English from Mills College. Having grown frustrated with the lack of relatable works in the English canon, her work seeks to center her own multifaceted identity as a daughter of the African Diaspora. Her job working with elementary school students has informed her desire to empower students with the tools they need to write their own stories. It is her hope that grabbing the past by its roots will nurture creative spirits of the future.

Jewell King-Speaks is a student at University of Ghana in Legon. He is the 2018 Jive Slam Champion and the winner of the 2016 Ehalakasa Slam in Ghana. He has performed in Cote d'Ivoire during the 2017 and 2018 BABI Slam festival and also in Port Harcourt, Nigeria for the Alive poetry show. He is the creator and artistic director of Handred Pesewas which presents poetry and acoustic music every January.

Joseph Chief Korgan, aka Wordrite, is a 21 year young man with the love of poetry embedded in his genes. A student of the university of Ghana and a part-time worker (cashier) at a koffee lounge, he has had the opportunity to bless several microphones from the Ehalakasa Festival, Nkabom Festival, Chalewote Festival, and a few poetry shows across the country. He loves to take words through a ritual where they transform from mere sounds to a series of insatiable ear-meals.

Sandra Hooper Mayfield, aka Makeda, is a poet, journalist, tutor, counselor, and community activist. She is best known for her work with youth. Makeda developed and served as editor of the South County publication of the Oakland Post. In 2006 she won the Ella Hill Hutch award for her contribution to journalism. Makeda's work is published in three Alameda County Seniors poetry anthologies and a chapbook collection. She developed the "Third Saturday Open Mic," and an annual artist retreat, Sugar Water.

Nathaniel Tetteh Ogli, with an Artiste name, Natty Ogli, is a Ghanaian Wordsmith using his gift as a reformative tool to contribute to positive change. Natty is a multitalented artiste, instrumentalist, singer, and rapper in the style of reggae/dancehall. As a member of Ehalakasa, his unique approach to Spoken Word Poetry exemplifies the tenacious pursuit of righteousness and truth.

Etchian Jean Frédéric Orbeli is a poet from Abidjan, Cote d'Ivoire.

Woédem Afua Parku, aka Woé, aka Z. Afua, is an Ewe Ghanaian story-teller whose work is a curation and documentation of Ewe culture, preservation of experiences, and creation of safe spaces. Her biannual intimate gathering, Nativity, is a narrative of personal and collective experiences centered on traumas, healing, and growth. Woé's work aims to explore narratives of culture, mental health, relationships, and spirituality as catalysts for nonconformity and healing.

Marcus Lorenzo Penn, aka Adeshima, is a native of the San Francisco Bay Area. In service to his many gifts as a holistic doctor, photographic artist, yoga teacher, wellness consultant, self-care coach, group facilitator, poet, author, and speaker, Dr. Penn is passionate about living, seeing, reflecting, moving through life fully, and helping others do the same. His travels have taken him to six continents, Prior to his 2018 visit to Ghana with WOWA, he also visited that nation in 2007.

Wanda Sabir is a journalist and author, moonlighting as a college professor in Alameda, California (wandaspicks.com). She is also a Depth Psychologist, with deep roots in the bayous of Louisiana where she was born. Her interests and expertise are historic trauma and trauma healing—the Maafa, specifically ancestral memories, dream tending, women prisoners, and the use of art to stimulate those forgotten conversations, especially among Diaspora descendants. She is co-founder of MAAFA San Francisco Bay Area, in its 25th Season October 2020 (maafasfbayarea.com), co-founder of The International Coalition for the Commemoration of African Ancestors of the Middle Passage (remembertheancestors.com) and recent recipient of the Distinguished 400 Award, 400 Years of African American History Commission (2019). She is a Transformative Justice (TJ) or Community Accountability facilitator and believes the true revolution starts at home. For thirty years, she has hosted the West Oakland Library: A Celebration of African American Writers and their Poetry.

Mariska Araba Taylor-Darko hails from Saltpond and Abura Wiomoa in the Central Region of Ghana. She is a published writer, poet, and a motivational speaker. She has published several books: *The Secret to Detoxifying Your Life* and *Love, Rhythms of Poetry in Motion, Vol. 1, The Iced Water Seller; The Deer Hunt;* and an eBook titled *A Widow Must Not Speak*. She is in the process of completing two children's books titled *King Goat Aponkye* and *Princess Afia the Warrior*. She is an executive member of the Ghana Association of Writers. She is the mother of two sons.

Crystal Tettey is an Artist, Curator and Arts-in-Development Consultant. Crystal currently facilitates a monthly literary series dubbed "Let's Talk Poetry." The series, set in the Library of Goethe-Institut Ghana, explores the experience(s) of Creative Persons via Conversation and Performance. She is also the Co-ordinator of Youth Leadership and Bilingual Support of the Africa Region for Special Olympics International (an organization that actively promotes the rights of Persons with Intellectual Disabilities).

Kathryn Waddell Takara, PhD, is a renowned poet and non-fiction author who penned the Afterword to this book. With a doctorate in Political Science, she has authored eight books of poetry, a collection of oral histories, and a scholarly biography. She is a winner of the American Book Award.

Imani Todd is currently in training as a Content App Reviewer to process apps created globally in the English language. She just finished her performance in Bakanal de Afrique's "What Had Happened Was," an Afro Urban Musical produced by the Afro Urban Society. Imani is furthering her involvement with Afro Urban Society, focusing on her dance career, and applying for future opportunities to travel abroad.

Tamaris Usher is a rapper from East Oakland. He graduated from Merritt College in the process of WO2WA.

Sir Black aka Yibor Kojo Yibor is a spoken word performance artist and workshop facilitator. He is a co-founder of Ehalakasa, a spoken word poetry community and director of the annual Ehalakasa Festival. He is involved in organizing spoken word poetry events, workshops, and youth development projects in schools and communities in collaboration with local, international, and cultural institutions. Yibor works across painting, sculpture, installation and spoken word poetry. Using text, sounds, images and objects, he is interested in exploring the notion of self-examination within three dimensions - Then, Now and After. His performances are characterized by the use of his body as the object and the ticking of time as subject. He lives and works in Ghana. He is a three-time prizewinner in spoken word poetry in Ghana.

About the Editor

 **Karla Brundage** is a Bay Area based poet, activist, and educator with a passion for social justice. Born in Berkeley, California, Karla spent most of her childhood in Hawaii where she developed a deep love of nature. She is the founder of West Oakland to West Africa Poetry Exchange (WO2WA), which has facilitated cross-cultural exchange between Oakland and West African poets. She is currently editing a pan-Africanist WO2WA poetry collection, *Our Spirits Carry Our Voices*, to be published by Pacific Raven Press in 2020. Karla is a board member of the Before Columbus Foundation, which provides recognition and a wider audience for the wealth of cultural and ethnic diversity that constitutes American writing. Her poetry book, *Swallowing Watermelons*, was published by Ishmael Reed Publishing Company in 2006. Her poetry, short stories and essays have been widely anthologized and can be found in Hip Mama, Literary Kitchen, Lotus Press, Bamboo Ridge Press, Vibe and Konch Literary Magazine. She holds an MA in Education from San Francisco State University and an MFA from Mills College.

Brundage has worked to bring light to many voices in her role as editor including the following texts:

Editor. *Words Upon the Waters: A Poetic Response to Hurricane Katrina* by Bay Area Writers and Artists. Oakland, CA: Jukebox Press, 2006.

Co-editor with Kim Shuck. *Oakland Out Loud: Poetry and Prose in Celebration of "There."* Oakland, CA: Jukebox Press, 2007.

Editor. *Jerri Lange: A Black Woman's Life in the Media.* Ishmael Reed Publishing Company. Oakland, CA: 2009.